STARTING OVER

STARTING OVER

THE SUCCESSES AND FAILURES OF 12 ENTREPENEURS LIKE YOU

Christian Korwan

1st edition, September 2020.
© Christian Korwan Consulting LLP, 2020.
Illustrations: Rita Baulies.
Editing: JL Servicios Editoriales.
Translation: Amber Aguilar.

About the author

Christian Korwan is a 49-year-old serial entrepreneur. He has founded over twenty companies in his lifetime; some of them of noteworthy success. In addition to managing his companies, among them the investment fund Nomad Kapital, he helps other entrepreneurs to achieve their aims and dreams, to grow their businesses, to create better services and products, and to generate jobs, wellbeing, and, of course, economic wealth.

To find out more about the author and to access free extra content, visit his website and sign up:

www.christiankorwan.com

Table of contents

Introduction

"Nothing is lost if you have the courage to proclaim that everything is lost and that you have **to start over**."

JULIO CORTÁZAR

12ᵗʰ May 2020.

I've been locked down in Madrid for two months: an eternity for a wanderer like me. In fact, if not for the virus, I'd be in Canada now, where some good friends are still waiting for me. But the coronavirus crisis caught me here, in my daughter Jacqui's apartment in Madrid, and here is where I'll have to stay.

Luckily, I can keep working. Well, not luckily. I can do it because I shaped my life to enable me to work and to direct my companies from anywhere in the world. This freedom is my greatest treasure. I carry my businesses around in my backpack, and I can move to any place in less than a day, even in just a few hours. For some people, not having a fixed place with firm roots is disconcerting. For me, it's life.

It hasn't always been that way. I've changed my values and priorities as time has gone on. I've "streamlined" my backpack, my personal baggage and my mental baggage. "Less is more," they say. I've applied that, and I love feeling so light. Now, what matters to me isn't having a fast car or a bigger house than the neighbors. Now what matters to me is having experiences: spending every moment where I want to be and with who I want to be with.

It's thanks to this minimalist and nomadic philosophy that I've found it so easy to adapt to the lockdown. I miss going out whenever I want and visiting friends, sure, and above all I miss traveling, but remote working is charted territory for me. I'm used to it; all I need is my cellphone, my laptop, an internet connection, and that's about it. With these meager resources, I've been able to continue advising my clients on their investments and business projects. Although none have considered withdrawing their investments from the fund I manage, Nomad Kapital, I have noticed some concern regarding the situation we're in right now. And it's logical: all the news we're hearing about the economy is negative. Unprecedented falls in GDP, the losses of millions of jobs, thousands of company closures...I just read an article about this last point that chilled me: "Over half a million small businesses won't reopen this year because of the coronavirus". This is a prediction from the Spanish Confederation of Small and Medium Enterprises (CEPYME).

Half a million companies is a lot of companies. And that's just in Spain alone! How many are disappearing in France, Italy, or the States?

I can't help thinking about the people behind those businesses: about their dreams, and about their sadness or anger when they have to pull down their shutters, literally or figuratively speaking. Sometimes, when we read the news, we forget that there are people behind every company: people with dreams, who fought to get their business where it is, who toss and turn at night when things go awry, when sales are down, when they fear for their future and that of their families...

Now, there are many people in that situation – many more than before this crisis. And I know exactly how they feel. Or how you feel, if you're among them.

I'm not just saying that. I too have experienced the anguish of business failure. It's a bitter pill, and it left me broke and homeless. It was in the early 00s, when the real estate boom was booming. I met an entrepreneur who, with no prior experience, had set up a gypsum plaster business: a niche that was gaining popularity at the time. It made me think that I could get into the construction sector, too, so I threw myself into setting up a renovation company. In under eighteen months, I had gone from having two workers to having thirty-two, and from renovating someone's yard to building a leisure center. But things suddenly went wrong. I had a non-payment worth €150,000, and I went under. I lost my company, my house, my car, and all my money. EVERYTHING. My daughter Jacqui, who was a little two-year-old at that point, was all that kept me going and gave me the strength to carry on. She hadn't asked to be there, she had nothing to do with the situation, and she deserved all my effort to get us back on track. She became my driving force, my daily motivation, my reason to keep fighting, to survive, to never give up...

I think back to that time, and it sends a chill down my spine. And my life has never been easy. I was orphaned at eighteen, having lost both my parents within the space of two years. My father had Alzheimer's, and my mother had battled cancer for six years. After that, I had to find work, and deal with tyrannical bosses who took advantage of me professionally, which wasn't easy either. But the moment I remember being toughest of all was when I had to hand over the keys to my house, leaving me with nowhere to live with my wife and daughter. That was the hardest thing of all.

That's why I can completely empathize with the situation of people fearing they will have to close down their business over all this. Many of them have stopped bringing in money, and they still have expenses. Many have had to lay people off. Many have had to make partial social security and tax payments. And even then, many of them – far too many – will never be able to reopen their doors, and they'll have to start over.

I wish I could reassure them, or even give them some idea to help them dust themselves off and keep going. I wonder what I can do, and for a moment, it occurs to me that I could write a book on my own experiences as an entrepreneur. Because my story doesn't end with the failure I just told you about; in fact, it starts there. After going under, I worked hard, built myself back up, and founded other businesses that did succeed: some were very successful indeed. And now, at forty-nine, I can say that I have the life I want and I want for nothing.

So, perhaps I have something to offer people who are in the position right now of not knowing how to react or what to do. However, I don't think my life is interesting enough to dedicate an entire book to. I could talk about a few interesting things (in fact, I'm pretty sure I'll do that over the coming pages), but not so much so that I could write memoirs or anything like that. Plus, I'm not trying to write a book talking about how amazing I am or how knowledgeable. It wouldn't feel right to do that. My aim is something else: to encourage and motivate entrepreneurs who have having a hard time right now, with ideas, proposals or truly useful experiences. To tell them they're not alone, that many of the people they see now online or on TV who have come out on top failed once, too, and kept going in spite of it.

And I have another idea. I think it just might work: to let other entrepreneurs tell me about their difficult times and how they got through them. Their failures and successes. I've been participating in various think tanks and forums about starting up businesses for years, so I've had the chance to meet a lot of entrepreneurs and business owners – and not just here in Spain, but from all over the world. In fact, my wanderlust and my talent for languages (I'm a native German speaker, and I also speak English and Spanish) has enabled me to make friends all over. Some of them are famous and others aren't, but I'm sure that they can all bring some very interesting ideas and experiences to the table.

I like this idea, but I do have one doubt. Though I have my own blog and I like writing, I've never written a book, and the thought of doing it is pretty daunting. I think I might need someone by my side throughout this process. I remember that once, at a roundtable event, I met Cipri Quintas, the author of *The Networking Book* (not yet available in English), and he told me about a writing coach he knew. I called Cipri, told him about my book idea, and he didn't miss a beat: "You need Josep López". And so, without further ado, he made one of his legendary conference calls.

All of a sudden, I find myself talking about the book with Cipri and Josep in a totally impromptu chat. As the minutes go by, the project begins to take shape. By the time I hang up, I'm totally convinced: I'm going to do this!

13th May 2020.

I've spoken to some entrepreneur friends of mine and the answer has been unanimous: they love the idea, and they want to be a part of it.

I started making a list: Juan Merodio, Jaime Chicheri, Cipri Quintas himself (who's been a business owner for over thirty years), bestselling author Marc Reklau, Jack Vincent, Julian Hosp (an Austrian living in Singapore with a fascinating story) ...

I like my list because it covers various nationalities, ages and backstories. But when I've finished it, I realize something: they're all men. This makes me wonder: don't women experience big business failures, or is it just that my professional circle is all-male? Is it possible that women are more careful or do business differently? I don't know — but what I do know is that a book like this needs to include women, both to answer those very questions for me and to provide a female perspective on running a business.

I ask my buddies Cipri and Josep about this. Several names come up, among them Judit Catalá and Mónica Mendoza. I contact the first of these and her response is enthusiastic — I've caught her right in the middle of moving, though, so we agree to talk in a few days, once she's settled in a little.

I contact everyone on my list. The first person to

get back to me is Juan Merodio: always with his finger on the pulse. He loves the idea and suggests having the interview the day after tomorrow on Zoom. Great! I hang up excited, but then I start to panic. What am I going to ask him? Should I delve into personal matters or keep it professional? What might interest potential readers of my book?

I decide to create a questionnaire this evening. I call Josep and together we create a list of questions:

- For those who don't know you, can you explain a little of your story as a person and as an entrepreneur?
- What has been your biggest failure? What happened and what was your experience as a result?
- Whose fault was it? Have you ever thought that it might have been yours, at least partly?
- How did you overcome it?
- How did you feel? Angry, scared, outraged?
- Did the failure affect your professional or personal life? In what way?
- What about your relationship with your partner?
- Did anyone help you? How?
- What did you learn from that experience?
- What would you never do again?
- Were you scared or reluctant to begin another business or project?
- If you were, how did you overcome that?
- After that experience, what new strategies or tactics do you apply?
- Have your priorities in life changed? Have your values changed?

- Looking back, is there anything you regret?
- Would you now do anything that you didn't do when it happened?
- What would you say to somebody going through a business failure right now?

I like it. I'm sure more questions will come up later, or I'll change some slightly, but we'll look at that as we go along. For now, I feel prepared.

Let's do this!

"

I too have experienced
the anguish of business
failure.
It's a bitter pill, and it
left me broke
and homeless.

JUAN MERODIO (1980)

www.juanmerodio.com
www.linkedin.com/in/juanmerodio

15th May 2020.

Today I've met with Juan Merodio to hold the first of twelve interviews I aim to do. I've been following Juan since before we met in person. For years, he's been a benchmark in the world of entrepreneurship and I've always liked to follow people who do it well, especially when what they say makes a lot of sense and they speak from experience. You can spot fakers and bullshitters a mile off; you can tell straight away when people are just repeating what they've heard. But Juan isn't like that: he's a born entrepreneur.

Despite his youth, at just forty years old, he's been setting up businesses for fifteen years. He's also a frequent speaker at conferences and teaches at some of the best business schools and universities. He's also a digital adviser for political candidates and governments, as well as a digital market consultant for companies in Spain, Latin America, the US and Canada. But, above all, he's an entrepreneur who started his first company at twenty-four, dedicated to creating websites focused on female audiences. Then he created more, such as InvierteME, a network for entrepreneurs and investors; Emprende Finance, which helps people starting businesses to secure funding for their projects; SocialVane, a developer of a smart monitor based on AI; UXBAN, a luxury housing development agency; Marketing Surfers, a digital marketing agency; Engage Worldwide, a company for digital business transformation for adapting to the new economy, with offices in Miami, Bogota and Toronto; and his namesake company, Juan Merodio, where he and his team develop business consultancies in marketing and digital transformation for companies worldwide.

He has also written nearly a dozen books on digital marketing, such as *9 Factors for the Digital Transformation of a Company*, *Marketing Content: How to Define your Strategy in 2018* and *The 20 Tools of Digital Marketing for your Business* (not yet available in English), among others.

We meet online at five o'clock in the evening. He's the first person I've interviewed, so I'm a little curious to see how it goes. We're both in casual wear: I'm wearing a light gray sweatshirt and he's in a white shirt with the sleeves rolled up, showing some braided bracelets on his left wrist and a black smartwatch on the right. There's no chitchat; we get straight to the point. I start by asking him about his personal story – the one that he doesn't put on his official resumes or on his LinkedIn profile.

JM: The first memory I have isn't really a memory, but something my dad told me about. Apparently, when I was three, I was given a remote control car, and instead of playing with it, I took it apart to see what was inside. Then I did the same with the rest of my toys, and other stuff, too. I always dismantled stuff, it was weird. I later found out that's a common trait among entrepreneurial people. We're curious. Another typical characteristic is that we like to build things. That's why I was a real lover of Mecano and Lego. We entrepreneurs like to create companies, products, teams and so on by starting from scratch.

CK: So, you knew from a very young age that you wanted to be an entrepreneur...

JM: I knew from early on that I didn't want to be ordered around. I didn't want to have a boss. I really don't get on with baseless authority: someone telling me what to do or giving me orders unless it's truly justified. I would talk back from a young age. Whenever my parents told me "do this", I'd ask, "why?". It must be because I'm scientifically-minded and I need to understand things.

CK: Were you like that at school, too?

JM: I ran into problems at school for being that way. I wasn't a brilliant student – I always passed by the skin of my teeth, just fulfilling requirements. And when it came to deciding what to study, I wasn't sure. I ended up doing Telecommunications Engineering in a private university, because I didn't pass my entrance exam. I carried on rebelling there, and it got me into trouble. From my very first class I was questioning everything. Teachers were afraid of me, because I was quite argumentative. As a consequence, I was asked to leave before I managed to graduate. It was really me who brought that about, because I didn't like Telecommunications and I didn't see myself working in it. Even though it was a course with some amazing avenues. I had classmates in their third year who were already working and earning three thousand euros a month. But it wasn't for me.

Juan gesticulates a lot with his arms, and he moves around constantly. While he's talking about his childhood and adolescence, he sits up and then leans back again several times, as if the office chair he's sitting in were electrified. He's a bundle of nerves, pure restlessness, constantly wanting to do things and convey things.

JM: So I quit the course without finishing, to my parents' disappointment. Then I thought about what to do and I started working on commission for a real estate company, Tecnocasa. I had no idea how to sell apartments, but I was a pretty fast learner. Not to blow my own trumpet, but I always have been. For example, I taught myself to play guitar, and at fourteen I was giving private lessons at home and getting a little pocket money that way. At twenty I was also earning, by trickery. There was an online photography competition that gave cash prizes to the most highly-voted pictures. I kept entering and winning – but not because I was good. It was because I'd invented a system that consisted of putting the cursor on "vote" and then leaving the mouse on the "enter" button so that it kept on pressing it in a loop. And since back then they didn't have IP filters, my photos were the most highly-voted by far. With what I earned in those few months (until they caught me, that is) I bought a motorbike and still had money left over... I mean, when I started out in real estate I thought I was learning on the job. And I was:

I started selling, selling, selling… But like I said, I can't stand having a boss, so I clashed with the owner of the company and ended up moving to another agency. I went through four real estate agencies and it always ended badly. For that very reason: because I couldn't stand being ordered around with no real justification. It's a good thing I didn't have to do military service; I would've ended up in the guardroom.

We laugh. I can just picture Juan asking the sergeant: "Hey, so why do we have to line up all together and wear the same thing? I think we should do it differently…" Military discipline isn't for him, that's for sure.

JM: After a few years of going from agency to agency in real estate, I decided to set up on my own. The problem was I knew nothing about business. I thought about doing a masters, but I didn't have a college degree, so I couldn't do one officially. I found a pretty prestigious business school in Madrid that had a masters in Marketing and Commercial Management, and they let me sign up because I had professional experience. I took out my first loan to pay for that course, which was a year and a half long and cost a bomb. I paid it off with what I got from selling apartments. Since I studied for the masters on Friday evenings and Saturday mornings, which are working days in real estate, I negotiated with my boss that I'd make up those hours during the week, so I went for a year and a half with basically no days off. I was the youngest person on the master's course. Most of them were directors of a certain age and a lot of experience. At first it was hard for me because I didn't understand anything. It was all Greek to me. But I knuckled down and rolled up my sleeves. Every day I'd spend five hours studying. And after six months, I had an idea and I set up my first business: a car website for women, www.ellasconducen.com.

CK: We entrepreneurs tend to remember our first business well, although they almost always end up going badly.

JM: Yeah, because you feel this special hope. In my case, I drew up a business plan, calculated that I needed fifteen thousand euros to get it going, and I went to the bank and took out a loan with my father's guarantee. They gave it to me and I hired a company to make the website for me. I did it all without telling the real estate agency anything; I was still working there and doing stuff to do with real estate marketing, so digital marketing was beginning to interest me. I held meetings for my new business at eight in the morning or eight at night, so that my work wouldn't suspect anything. They were a very traditional company and wouldn't have allowed me to do two things at once. I juggled the two jobs for a year until I'd broken even on the fifteen thousand and then I decided to go for it. That was the moment I took the leap. Oddly, it was right when the real estate crash was beginning.

CK: Did the crisis of 2008 affect you in any way?

JM: It did, but in my favor. I don't know why, but crises work for me. In fact, I've become a specialist at setting up companies that work well in times of crisis. I guess it's because as they say, there are big opportunities in every crisis. Some people go bankrupt, some people become millionaires. And in the middle are some big opportunities for normal people like us.

The question is how to detect them and go after them.

CK: What problems did you face at the start?

JM: I was working from home and freelancing, so some people told me I wasn't projecting a professional image. What's more, I was working in the world of cars and I was a petrolhead, yet I was driving around in a souped-up Ford Fiesta in a messed up condition. When I would go to meetings, I had to park around the corner so no one would see it. I had no money, and what little I had got invested in training and moving the company forward. But I held my nerve and I got some big clients, like Mapfre.

CK: Where were you getting your income from?

JM: From advertising and through agreements with dealerships for giving them leads. The problem was that 80% of my income was coming from a single client, and when I had to renew contracts, which was usually in July, I was sweating. So I started some side businesses to try to diversify, like a network of websites for women on different topics: www.ellastrabajan.com, www.ellasviajan.com, about work and travel respectively, and others. From there, I set up a digital marketing agency mostly focused around women's stuff.

CK: Would you say that security for an entrepreneur comes from diversifying, from not limiting themselves to just one project?

JM: Some investors say you should just concentrate on one project and grow that, but that's risky for entrepreneurs. You need to look at each case individually, of course, but diversifying gives you a little leeway. It's normal for some things to work out and others not to. As well as diversifying, I think it's important to have an investment mindset, not a spending one. We freelancers have a bad habit of not differentiating between personal money and company money. Since you don't get a paycheck, it all gets mixed up. But my dad, who was the director of the publishing house Planeta and who's really good with finance stuff, taught me to separate the two so that I always know what I have. And I still do it that way, helped by my dad, who cooperates with me financially on my companies. He's been a key figure for me. I've always had several checking accounts, each one for a different thing: one for taxes, one for savings, one for investment, one for spending…And I can tell you one thing: I still live on the same amount of money as when I founded the company fifteen years ago. I earn more now, of course, but my mindset is still the same: keep reinvesting, instead of spending more.

CK: I think that's been one of my problems. I went self-employed in 1990, and I've never been able to separate my pay from my other expenses and investments. And when things have gone wrong, that's been a source of worry to me. I think it's a pertinent issue for lots of entrepreneurs.

JM: Yeah, for sure. As I said, I learned it early on from my dad, and it's been so useful to keep everything in its place.

CK: Let's talk a little about what I want the book to focus on: failures. Have you ever had a big one as an entrepreneur? What is your view on failure?

JM: Not so much one big failure, but I have several small ones. I remember a project I was working on for years, a jobseeking portal for women. Only after I'd spent a bunch of money developing it did I realize it

"

Juan Merodio: I don't know why, but crises work for me. In fact, I've become a specialist at setting up companies that work well in times of crisis. I guess it's because as they say, there are big opportunities in every crisis.

wasn't going to work. I had a dilemma: keep going, running the risk of losing more money, or writing off everything I'd invested in it over those years. And it hurt, but I went for the latter option. Since then, there's one thing I always do: when I start a new project, I establish how much money and how much time I'm prepared to invest in it. And I set myself a deadline, which I stick to no matter what. For example, I was in Canada, setting up a really great project, but six months in, I abandoned the idea. It was a shame, but it was a good call, because right after that I started work on another project, a real estate agency in Spain, and it worked out great. And that was because I called time on the other project before it was too late.

CK: Do you think failure is necessary for an entrepreneur?

JM: No, I don't subscribe to the school of thought that you have to fail in order to learn. Logically, you do learn from failure – but you learn from success, too. And given the choice, I'd rather learn from success than from failure. The thing is: to be successful, you sometimes have to overcome obstacles that throw you off course. It's like sailing into the wind: you can't go in a straight line. You have to zigzag around, correcting your course to get to your destination.

CK: What do you think has been your key to not having any big failures?

JM: I think it's because I've always lived within my means. It's like what I was saying before: even though I earn more, I don't spend more – I save it for a rainy day. When I was younger, I had friends who would spend 60% of their monthly income on car repayments. Personally, even though I love cars, I've always applied one strict rule: car repayments can't be more than 5% of my salary. If it's more, you're living outside your means. Either your car is too expensive or you don't earn much. Another key is not to get swept up by emotion. I'm not sentimental when I do business. If I have to abandon a project, I just do it and move on. I'm not proud, and I don't spend a long time moping. I'm a Gemini, so when I stop doing something, I just stop doing it and I don't give it any more of my energy. I'm also lucky enough to have a bad memory, so I quickly forget failures. I reset fast. The third key thing is that my discipline and persistence, even sometimes getting a little obsessive, has helped me stay focused. And the fourth thing is having had my father by my side. Not just because he took care of financial stuff, which is an area I don't like, but because I can share my concerns with him any time. One of the biggest handicaps for entrepreneurs is often loneliness: not having anyone to share your worries or your doubts with. It's not easy to find someone you can explain them to and they'll help. But my dad has helped me a lot and still does; he gives me good advice on managing teams and other day-to-day aspects. It's also so, so important to have the support of Vicky, my wife. Sometimes, entrepreneurs aren't supported by the people closest to them, but I'm lucky enough that I do. My wife is amazing, and her support gives me a lot of confidence. We share the same life views and I'm really lucky in that sense.

CK: I agree with what you say about the loneliness of the entrepreneur. It's important to have someone with you who can listen to you and advise you. In my case, I have Lau: she's my right hand, and has carte blanche to stop me if at any point I go a little crazy with too many projects, or if she thinks I'm losing my way. It's fundamental to be around people who add things rather than taking them away. Positive people – not toxic ones. I really believe that we are the five people we spend the most time with.

JM: Yes, that's totally true. Although you make your own decisions. In my case, as I said, my dad has been a good adviser, but I've always done what I thought I had to do, even when I was little, like I was telling you before. One of my mantras is: "Hear what everyone says but don't listen to any of it." If I had listened to my parents, I wouldn't have started a business or got to where I am today. So while it's good to have your parents' support, you don't always have to listen to what they say. You have to choose your own path. I do what I want, when I want, how I want and where I want.

CK: And that's exactly how I define success!

JM: I'm with you on that. For me, success is getting up every morning and feeling that I'm free, and that I do what I do because I want to.

CK: Going on to something else, you say you don't like the finance part. Do you think it's better to correct your weaknesses, or nurture your strengths?

JM: I think you should work out what you're good at and foster that. Try to be the best at what you're good at. And the stuff you're not good at, you can learn, but since you'll never excel at it, the best thing to do is surround yourself with people who do. Everyone should know where they should be and take that responsibility. An entrepreneur's responsibility is to exploit their strengths and seek help with their weaknesses. And not to blame anybody for their failures.

CK: Have you ever blamed anyone else for your failure?

JM: No. Whether things go well or badly, the responsibility for that is mine. It's true there are some aspects you can't control, like a virus appearing that causes a worldwide crisis, but I don't focus on the things that aren't within my power to control. I only worry about what I can control. And I really go with my intuition. Over time, I've seen that when I go with my gut, I get more hits than misses. And I recently discovered that this has a scientific explanation, because your gut feeling is all your prior experiences boiled down.

CK: It sounds like you're a real pragmatist.

JM: Yeah. Yes, I'm very pragmatic. I always apply this: "If you can do something about it, why worry? If you can't do anything about it, why worry?" And you can't overthink things, either. You have to be quick. Ultimately, you don't know if something will work until you try it. In that sense, I'm not a perfectionist at all: I move at breakneck speed. My team helps me out with the details, because I just throw myself into it and correct things as I go along. I'm someone who prefers to apologize later than to ask for permission now. In fact, I don't ask for permission. With time and experience, I've learned to be more strategic, but I place a lot of focus on doing.

CK: Have you ever been afraid you'd fail?

JM: No, because I've never gotten into anything that wasn't painstakingly planned out, or in anything risky enough to leave my family out on the street. I've been pretty cautious, because I think when you have your financial situation under control, you can think more clearly. Plus, I've always accepted that businesses last for a while, not forever. They're like waves on the sea. It's true that, even if you take precautions, things can still suddenly fall apart – but worst case scenario and I go broke, I'm still young and I'd have time to get back on my feet. It's different if you're a little older.

As I listen to Juan, I think about how, though it's true that age makes a difference when it comes to starting businesses and investing, each case is different. For example, despite his young age, he's always been a careful guy – while some people never are, even when they're older. What does make a difference, when you're self-employed, is retirement. In my case, I'm running a fairly high risk right now, because I'm trying to build my own retirement without input from the State, since I don't trust it in the slightest. And since I'm nearly fifty, that means I have to risk a little more than is probably sensible for someone my age. As the saying goes: every man is a world unto himself.

Juan continues with his explanation:

JM: Rather than fear, what I feel is that I would be really annoyed if I couldn't get a project I was excited about to work. I mean, I'll be really annoyed if I don't live to be a hundred and fifty, because I have so many projects still in mind. But the only thing I'm afraid of is losing my health or someone I love losing their health. If you don't have your health, you don't have anything. I don't know what will happen further ahead. They say that when you turn forty, you get more fearful and become more conservative. But I'm not sure that's true.

Harland David Sanders, for example, founded Kentucky Fried Chicken at sixty years old.

CK: What is your latest project, if you can talk about it?

JM: It's an online school for training people in digital skills. I just launched it this week – like, right in the middle of the Covid-19 crisis. Like I was saying before, crises don't hold me back. I really believe in training: it changes everything. Whenever I've trained in a professional field, I've noticed an improvement in my life. I'm convinced that education is going to undergo huge changes, because doing a masters isn't currently accessible for everyone. What I want to achieve is for it to be possible for pretty much anyone in the world to access my masters.

CK: Speaking of education, do you think having a good education prevents failure?

JM: It's not a hundred per cent guaranteed, but it drastically improves your chances of success, without a doubt. Some entrepreneurs have created empires without even a basic education, but they're a minority. If you want to start a successful business, you have to invest in yourself. If you don't, you're lost. And especially so now. Maybe in my parents' time, not so much, but now... Also, you have to keep training. Something I've been doing for years, which I recommend to a lot of people, is setting an annual budget for training. A hundred, two hundred, a thousand, whatever you can: but do it every year, and make it a habit. If you don't, you're dead in the water.

CK: Knowledge is power.

JM: Totally. Many businesses fail because of a lack

of knowledge. If you set up an online store without the slightest idea about digital marketing, you're probably going to fail. But with some basic knowledge, your chances of success go right up. That's why the initial training I'm preparing is specifically about setting up an online business. In twelve weeks, I'm going to teach people how to get a business going from scratch. With just that knowledge, the chances of success are great.

CK: Are you concerned with leaving a legacy?

JM: Yes, that motivates me more than the money. When I'm an old man, I'd love for someone to study digital marketing and see my name and my experience come up. And for that to help some people. In fact, 90% of the content I publish is free; I don't get any income from it. But I don't care, because I know there are people out there benefitting from it. Obviously, someone setting up a business wants to make money, but it's not my main driving factor. When you do something just for the money, sooner or later, you'll run into problems.

CK: What do you still need to do?

JM: Oh, lots of things. Learn astronomy, learn to play piano... In fact, everything I'm doing now is part of a plan: to retire at forty-five. Or – I should say – to have the infrastructure and the means to be able to work just four or five hours a day, and spend the rest of my time doing all the things I haven't been able to do so far because I've been so into my companies.

CK: Finally, what would you say to someone who's going through a difficult time with their business right now?

JM: I'd tell them to try to keep perspective: reality

is usually not as good or as bad as we think it is. I'd tell them to try to break the vicious cycle of negative thoughts, because all that does is attract more negativity. It's a good time to reduce costs to the bare essentials and analyze what past decisions led them to this point. Because, as I was saying before, ultimately the responsibility falls to the individual person. We can't go around blaming others. And, of course, I'd tell them that this too shall pass. They've been through other difficult or dramatic situations in their lives, from relationship breakups to losing loved ones. Except for very extreme cases, everything passes.

We've now been talking for an hour and a half. I've really identified with Juan on a lot of things, like his optimism, his views on success, and his aversion to having a boss – which I think is a very common trait among entrepreneurs. In my case, I worked for myself for eight years, between the ages of nineteen and twenty-seven, before I started my own serious business. I only ever had three bosses. The first was a German businessman in Tenerife who I knew through my mother. He had an electronics company. He was a good manager, but he had a bad habit of chewing out his staff. The second was a bully who was always arguing with people and owing them money; though I have to admit he was a great salesman, and, in his own way, a real fighter. The third and last, who owned a promotional outings company, had a drinking problem – he didn't know his own limits, and made the mistake of risking his family's inheritance on a single business. I learned something from each of them: mainly about what not to do.

I don't want to take up any more of Juan's time, so I thank him for his generosity and honesty, and we say goodbye with a virtual hug – the only kind available right now. We agree to meet up soon in Madrid – if possible, at Silk, the restaurant of our mutual friend Cipri Quintas, another superentrepreneur and one I have an appointment to speak with tomorrow.

"

Juan Merodio: Many businesses fail because of a lack of knowledge. If you set up an online store without the slightest idea about digital marketing, you're probably going to fail.

"

CIPRI QUINTAS (1966)

www.cipriquintas.com
LinkedIn: www.linkedin.com/in/cipriquintas

16ᵗʰ May 2020.

I only met Cipri in person a little while ago, but it feels as if we've known each other our whole lives. We really clicked. I read his bestseller, *The Networking Book,* recently, and shortly afterwards we attended the same conference. It was there that I discovered he is just as he presents himself in his book: the real McCoy. Sincere and charming, he's a bundle of affection. And of words! I don't know many people who like to talk more than I do, but Cipri is one of them. Our phone calls last at least an hour and half. That's why I'm sure my interview with him will be long and packed with content.

Cipri is one of the people who most encouraged me to write this book. Ever since I explained the idea to him, he hasn't stopped sending me contacts from his full address book. And, of course, he's going to be an interviewee, too – not just as a networking expert, but as a longstanding businessman. His many years of experience aren't because he's old; they're because he started very, very young. He had a lot of success with several nightclubs, and, more recently, with numerous restaurants, including Silk and Bang Cook Foundation.

Like me, he's in Madrid – specifically, in Alcobendas – but the lockdown means we can't meet in person. We'll just have to hold the interview over Zoom. We get online and I notice the quality of the image is really good – better than usual. I ask him what camera he's using, and his answer surprises me: it's his iPhone.

CQ: Yeah, it's great. The quality is amazing. But wait: I'm just going to put it on do not disturb, because if I don't, people will keep calling me and we'll get distracted… Okay, good to go.

CK: Great. Well, to start with, I'd like you to tell me a little about who Cipri Quintas is. I know you, but some readers of the book might not.

CQ: I've been a businessman for over thirty years, but as well as that, I've always been interested in people and relationships. That's the most important thing in the world for me. I grew up in San Sebastián de los Reyes, near Madrid, and I've always been a hometown boy. My dad was in the Spanish military police and in the evenings he worked in a little mechanic's workshop to get some extra money, because his salary didn't go far. Like my mother, he was a humble person, simple. He tried to get me to study, but I was never a good student. I've always been too flighty; I got distracted so easily. I learned very valuable things from him. I learned you have to keep your word, be honest and have values: don't steal, don't lie and try to be a good person. My mother is still alive, and she's an angel. She was also looking after people who got sick in our town or seeing if there was someone to help. When I earned some money, I bought them an apartment in another neighborhood, because they were getting old and they didn't have an elevator. And a lot of people cried when my mother left. She's a well-loved woman... We weren't a culturally educated family, but we had a lot of love. So when I started at college, I could see I wasn't going to pass, so I made friends with the principal. It was natural, not something I forced. But since then I've always done the same thing: won people's hearts. I don't know much about anything, but I have the phone numbers of people who do know, and since they like me, they always pick up when I call.

CK: That's great!

CQ: I think the most important thing for doing well in life is investing in people's hearts. But invest naturally, without expecting anything in return. Because when you do, you get a lot more back than what you give. I wasn't a handsome kid, nor was I athletic or intellectual, so I developed the art of getting on well with people. I'm sure I've just anticipated other questions you'll ask me later, but it has to do with what I'm telling you about the college principal. His name was José Luis González Quirós. I always organized the end-of-year trips, workadays, anything other than studying. And since I was always involved in that stuff, I had a real connection with him. One day he explained to me that he had designed a perpetual diary. Back then diaries were annual and on paper, so they stopped being useful when the year was up. He had designed one that you could keep adding sheets to, so it never expired. He suggested to me setting up a business and for me to be in charge of selling the diary. I didn't even know what one was, but I said yes. I bought a suit and, since I had just passed my driver's test and had no car, he lent me his to go round selling. People started calling my house with orders, because back then we didn't have cellphones, and my mom would tell them they had the wrong number – because she didn't know I'd set up a business. My dad found out and told me to keep studying, but I'd already decided I wasn't going to get anywhere by studying. Plus, I was convinced the diary thing was going to be a success. My mom helped me make a prototype using an old pair of jeans, because we didn't have any leather, and I went round all the paper shops in central Madrid with it. The only suit I had was a winter one, so when the weather got hot, I was sweating like a pig. But I wore my suit and carried my briefcase, which a friend had gifted me, and I felt like the king of the world. The college principal had a contact and got me a meeting with Isidoro Álvarez, ex-president of the El Corte Inglés department stores. I had no idea who he was. They ordered two thousand diaries from us and I left his office jumping for joy. The problem was that we made them, and they returned them to us, saying the leather we had used wasn't the one they had ordered. The college principal – by then my partner – gave me such a ticking off. I felt like the world's unluckiest guy. It was a disaster. I remember that summer's day, standing on a bridge over the M30 highway, my briefcase in hand, sweating buckets and thinking: "My life is pointless, why did I get into this, I'm just a poor guy from the neighborhood, what was I thinking…I'm gonna jump off the bridge, I can't take this." I wasn't really going to kill myself, obviously. Plus, I was sweating so much that even the thought of suicide sounded uncomfortably. The sweat was running down inside my pants…"

CK: Hahaha.

CQ: So I went to a phone booth and called the purchasing manager at El Corte Inglés. I explained the situation to him, and he felt so sorry for me that he ended up keeping the diaries. "But," he told me, "you have to promise that when you get paid for the diaries, you have to come back to El Corte Inglés and buy yourself a summer suit. You can't wear that one any more." So I did. And when I went to buy the suit, I dropped by his office and left the tags with his secretary, who couldn't stop laughing, so that he'd see I'd kept my word. So that's the story of my first failure, and, in a way, my first success.

CK: That's great!

CQ: I think the key was honesty. It's something I've always tried to maintain. Even when I did my military service. I could have gotten out of it because I had health issues, but it wasn't that serious, so I was honest and I said I wanted to do it. Anyway, being the son of military police and loving my country like I do, I would've been ashamed my whole life if I hadn't. I won't tell you my army stories, because I'll bore you, but I can promise you there are stories to tell. But I came back after a year and I had to start my life over. I started out as a DJ's assistant at a nightclub, and then I became a DJ. It went great. I didn't actually know how to DJ, but every time I changed the disc I would say something in made-up English into the mic, and people went crazy for it. Then I convinced the owners of an old movie theater to convert it into a nightclub. My friend Luis Lucena and I partnered up with the family that owned it, and we turned it into a club that ended up being legendary among young people of the time in Madrid: Desguace. The name, which means scrapyard, came about because we decorated it the cheapest way we could think of: with scrapped car parts. Some scrap metal booths and tacky lighting, and we had our nightclub. Without realizing it, we had created a new concept of shabby chic, purely because we were doing it with no money. But it was a runaway success: overnight, we had two thousand people queueing to get in. I had become a businessman without knowing how. To give you an idea of how clueless we were, at first we had to do the cleaning ourselves, because neither of us had thought to hire someone to do it.

CK: I love that.

CQ: It had its bad side, too. The first fights, the first heavies, the first problems with drug dealers, and so on. We were all just kids, even the bouncers. I gave them all suits so that they'd look more serious and command some respect. We had to learn on the job and with the resources we had. But the concept caught on and we became Madrid's favorite nightclub. It was partly luck; I have to admit. Since we didn't have any money to decorate, and the place was huge, we stuck two or three scrapped cars in the middle of the dancefloor and people thought that was awesome. Since we couldn't open at night, we opened in the evening, and evening parties became a thing. The floor was slippery, so we had a guy tossing sawdust on the floor the whole time, and people thought it was part of the décor. We invented a bunch of things, but purely to survive.

CK: And what was your next step?

CQ: More clubs. There was a bingo hall next to Desguace, and the owners suggested setting up something there. We created a restaurant-bar. Again, we had no decorating budget, so I went to a place where they made scale models and I asked them to let us have some in return for exposure. And they said yes. But it was all improve, totally chaotic, so we called the new place Kaos. And it was another total hit! Since it was tied to Desguace we decided to knock down a party wall to join the premises together, but then we found out we couldn't do it, because they were two separate buildings. Like I said: chaos.

CK: And did you carry on in the nightlife industry?

CQ: Yeah, then we set up Arrasa and a few more clubs. In total, alongside my associates, we opened around thirty. They weren't all nightclubs: we had a lounge, bars, restaurants, and so on. I ended up with four hundred workers with my partner José Luis Alonso, a great lawyer and economist, but for me above all a great life companion who I owe a lot to. He's one of my dearest friends. Without him, and other partners I've had over the course of my life, I wouldn't have achieved anything. Some projects failed, like Costa Desguace and Ozonia, and I lost a lot of money. This latter one was a mega-nightclub: the biggest in Spain, when we opened it. We took a huge knock for it, too. Another failure was the renovations and decoration company I set up, thinking it would save me money when opening clubs. Big mistake. It was right in the middle of the real estate boom, and salaries for construction workers were through the roof. When I saw how much framers and bricklayers were earning, I realized it wasn't going to work. But by then I'd sunk a lot of money into it. The same thing happened to me with a publishing house, a ballet studio, and more. Until I learned it's always better and cheaper to hire a professional who knows about each field. Another disastrous venture was the nightclub we opened in Gandía, in Valencia. I was bored one summer and I didn't know how to take a break, so we opened a nightclub on the coast, which we called Calle del Ritmo. It was huge: it had twenty-five bars. I thought: "This way, I can work and go for a dip while I'm there". Another mistake. We kept at it for seven years, and it never took off. And I went swimming twice in total! It was a mess. Plus, we had to deal with drug dealers, and I got several death threats for refusing to let them deal at the club. I've always been anti-drug and alcohol abuse, even if that seems weird for a nightclub owner. I remember in 1989, the newspaper ABC did an article on us: "Nightclub owners who fight against drug and alcohol abuse". And I thought, "how can this be news? It should be the norm…" In fact, I haven't touched a drop in ten years. Now I only drink wine because I'm friends with some excellent wine producers and I don't want to offend them. So, just to be friendly.

CK: How old were you when you had all the nightclubs?

CQ: I started at twenty-one. By twenty-six, I had a hundred million old pesetas, which was a lot of money back then. That said, I could give two shits about luxury. I was driving a 2CV and living with my parents. What I really wanted to do was start projects, have fun, and see people enjoying themselves in our clubs. That was what made me happy; not the money. In fact, I never had money, because I reinvested it all. Plus, my parents were religious and I'd grown up with the Christian culture of sacrifice, so I sacrificed myself and never allowed myself any treats. I became a millionaire not through what I earned, but through what I didn't spend.

CK: And you were never tempted to buy yourself a huge car or anything?

CQ: I bought a red Opel Calibra when my girlfriend, Maite, left me. She'd always told me I was stingy with myself. The first twenty-five miles I did were just crawling around her block so she'd see me. I didn't even care about the car; I just wanted her to see me in it.

CK: We were talking about Valencia and got off track...

CQ: Oh, yeah. I had a bad time there. Those were seven rough years. I don't know how I didn't get killed. But I was clear on who the good guys and bad guys were. I've always been clear on that. And I'm also very clear on that I side with the good guys. Trying to be bad doesn't solve anything; there's always somebody tougher, stronger, or badder than you. But anyway, they were difficult years. I lose a huge amount of money – around seventy million pesetas, which was a lot back in the nineties. I remember the day I talked to my associate there and told him to pay me whatever he thought and to keep the thing. He gave me an envelope with less than two per cent of what we'd invested. Me and my partner José Luis took the car and drove all the way to Madrid feeling depressed.

CK: Did you feel like you had that day on the bridge above the M30?

CQ: Worse! Because for me, failure isn't me feeling bad, it's other people feeling bad. Failure for me is when you have a nightclub, and suddenly you're standing in a hospital room, because two people had a fight and one of them is in a coma. Failure is when you leave your nightclub and see a road accident half a mile later and it turns out a guy got stoned at your club and crashed. And failure is when you can't make rent and you have to shutter down and fire people. I've had a few of those. I remember one that was particularly painful: a club called Café de Braganza, in central Madrid. It was twenty years ago. We found a great place on a street called Bárbara de Braganza that led from the Recoletos region of Madrid. We opened a little restaurant upstairs with a dancefloor downstairs. And it didn't work, because people were telling us: "No, I don't eat in the same place I drink and dance." We had to close and I lost a heap of money. And four or five years later, it became fashionable to have dinner and drink in the same place. We were visionaries, but too early on. When you're a pioneer, you need a lot of financial muscle to help you hold out, or you're screwed. You have to calculate if you can afford to be the first to do it: if you can wait it out. If you can't, it's better to be the third to do it.

CK: How did you overcome that failure?

CQ: Same way as any of them: by looking to the future and finding new projects. I've never been afraid to take risks. In fact, I've failed at lots of businesses, like the construction one, or a music label I set up too. If I could get back all the money I've lost on projects, I'd be one of the richest men in Spain [he laughs]. But fortunately, my successes have covered my failures. I've had to work very hard at some of them. For example, after the knock we took in Valencia, the social media boom started – I'm talking 2005, around then. And I could see it was going to be big. We set up a company, Valor de Ley (www.valordeley.es) with Antonio Moulet, the ex-president of NEC Ibérica, which no one believed in at first – but after four years of trial and error, and learning about the world of social networking, SEO and marketing, we got it off the ground. Today, it's a company of thirty people, and it's at the forefront of social media management. As I said, not many people believed in it at the start, especially because the whole social network thing was still cutting its teeth. People used social media to chat to friends, but they didn't realize how transcendent it would be. And gradually, with a lot of hard work, we carved out a place for our company, which is now an industry leader.

CK: But you work mostly in hospitality, right?

CQ: Yeah, but I've always got my fingers in a lot of pies. As a businessman, I'm a partner in a company that has a restaurant-nightclub in Alcobendas, Silk, and a restaurant in central Madrid, Bang Cook Foundation. Also, as I was saying, I have Valor de Ley, the digital marketing agency. But what I really like doing is starting projects and putting people in touch to make good things happen. I've been part of projects like that – mostly with friends of mine – but normally I just put them in touch with each other to work together because I know they'll get on. That's a phrase or slogan that really defines: "Make things happen". At Silk, we have it written on one wall: "Things happen here". I do it just for the pleasure of seeing new relationships emerge, new businesses, new projects. I'm not looking to profit. In fact, if I did, I don't think it would work.

CK: Were the big club in Valencia and the Café de Braganza your biggest failures?

CQ: Probably, but I never stop to count my losses or gains. It's not what really motivates me. If you asked me how much money I have right now, I wouldn't be able to tell you – I can promise you it's not much, though. I've never really kept up-to-date with my accounts; I've always had people to do it for me. Or partners who've taken care of that end of things, like my good buddy José Luis, to whom I owe so much. I just function differently. I don't even have a computer; I use my iPhone for everything. And I own a digital marketing company! I'm not saying it's the best way to do it, but I'm just like that: good at some things and not at others. My way of seeing business is so diffuse, so different...sometimes I come out on top for precisely that reason, but other times I don't. That I haven't made more money than I have is because I haven't tried hard to – I live the same way with a lot of money as I do with a little. And because life isn't about what you have, but what you give and what you do. My aim isn't to earn money, but to leave a mark on people's hearts, to leave a legacy, to grow for the better.

CK: And what has been your biggest business success?

CQ: I don't know if you can consider it a success, but I'm particularly fond of Silk, because we've been holding on for fourteen years. We opened before the 2008 crisis and the first few years went amazingly. A chic restaurant with a nightclub where the players of Real Madrid and lots of other celebrities would come, and it became Madrid's trendiest spot. But then the crisis happened and everywhere emptied out, and we had to reinvent ourselves several times. But we didn't fire anyone. Practically all the same people are working there who were there fourteen years ago. In fact, there are people who have been working with me for over thirty years. For me, Silk is more than a business: it was a life lesson. The learning has been so powerful that, no matter what happens in the future, I could never consider it a failure. Even though right now, with the Covid-19 crisis, we're having a terrible time of it. And there's more to come… But speaking of success, for me, my greatest success is having the friends I have. I'm the sum of all my friends.

CK: That reminds me of a phrase I really like: "We are the five people we spend most time with". I said it yesterday to Juan Merodio.

CQ: Well, if that's true, I must be amazing, because I spend a lot of time with my friends and they're all brilliant at what they do. That's what motivated me to write *The Networking Book* – not because I'm a guru at it, but because I have a wonderful network of friends. I'm hardwired to give, to connect with people, to connect other people with each other. But that's just because I have a calling for it and a lot of practice. In reality, anyone can do it with a little training.

CK: I really relate to a lot of the things you say. I'm listening to you and thinking: "He's talking about me!" Especially what you say about your motivations. I feel the same way as you. What matters to me isn't so much if a business is more or less profitable, but the life experience it brings me and the happiness it can bring to other people. Of course, the numbers have to be there, but that's not the most important thing... Sorry; I'm talking about myself. Tell me, where does your calling to help people come from, to make good things happen, as you say?

CQ: For sure it's from my mother. She's very devout and very generous. Some people might think giving has nothing to do with business, but for me, the best business is giving. To give is to add: it's to turn yourself into part of the solution, rather than being part of the problem. It's investing in people's hearts. Jesus Christ built his brand around giving – I mean that respectfully. And we're still talking about him two thousand years later! He was the world champion of giving, and I try to carry that in my world, my companies, my relationships. Because giving is the best tool we have today for building a personal brand. But you have to do it from your heart for it to truly work. My hashtag is #networkingconcorazón (networking with a heart), which begins with looking around you and seeing who you can help, not who can help you.

We stop briefly, because an alarm goes off on Cipri's cellphone to remind him he has another meeting shortly. He has actually already answered most of the questions I was planning to ask, but it would be great for the book if we could talk a little longer.

CQ: Sure, don't worry, we can keep going. I had an Insta Live, but they moved it for me.

CK: Great, thank you. I'd like to ask you about the topic of responsibility for failure. Do you think it was yours, or other people's?

CQ: In my case, I blamed other people for a while, because it helped me deal with it and because my ego couldn't accept failure. After a little time passed, I realized I hadn't been fair and I said sorry to those people. Now I've matured and I realize that it was all in my hands and I simply made mistakes. The movement came from me. I've also discovered that it's a real privilege to have the chance to mess up and fail. The important thing, if you make a mistake, is to be able to say you're sorry, ask for forgiveness and foster quality connections with people. Because the biggest failure is not being able to create those connections.

CK: Awesome.

CQ: There's a fable I love. It's the one about a guy walking in the desert carrying a canteen and a shovel in his rucksack. He's crossing the desert, wondering what the shovel could be for. When he runs out of water, he almost dies of thirst, until it occurs to him to dig with the shovel. He digs and digs until he hits a well. So he drinks, and feels better. He fills his canteen and goes on his way, but then he stops and thinks: "What if I run out of water again? Could there be a way to take all the water from the well with me?" But he can't think of anything. Just then, another man walks past, and the guy offers him water. And they become friends. And more and more people pass by and join together, and together they create an oasis... The moral of the story: we each have a shovel and we can create an oasis of people around us, but we're too lazy, and we'd rather keep on walking and let someone else dig the oasis. Grab your shovel and dig, man! Don't you see how amazing it is to create an oasis with your own hands? Don't you see that you'll never feel alone again in your life? Don't you see that other people will follow your example and dig too, and in the end, the oasis will be a paradise?

CK: That's so good!

CQ: In truth, despite everything I've told you, I don't really feel that I've ever failed at all – because I've always had a lot of people around me who were prepared to help me, a lot of friends I could call on in hard time.

Cipri is a whirlwind – he doesn't stop for a second, even in lockdown. He expresses himself so quickly – as soon as something pops into his head, he says it, no filter. And he smiles all the time. I think a key thing for someone to be so well-liked is to always have a smile, a joke or a caring word on their lips.

CK: How can you keep going with such a high level of activity?

CQ: I'm always short on time to do things, so I go to bed really late. Midnight comes and people are going to sleep, and I'm thinking: "The day can't end yet, I still have so much to do." I'm incapable of being still for a whole minute. I've been told more than once that I should meditate, but I can't – it's impossible. The only time I do anything close to meditating is when I go out running.

CK: What have you learned from your business failures?

CQ: A lot of things, but one above all: never do business with bad people, people who don't take care of their parents, their kids or their friends. Never do business with bad guys, because they'll always be bad. Nobility and honor above all, even above financial profit. I want to walk with people who are walking alongside me, no in front, because they'll block my way and I won't be able to see where I'm going. I don't want to be watching someone's ass as I walk, or for someone behind me watching mine. I want good people I can progress with, together. I've always identified with people I care about. That's my great freedom.

CK: That's part of my definition of success: being able to choose who you're with and who you spend your time with. Not being forced to spend it with people you don't like. Because the most valuable thing we own is our time, and wasting it with people who bring you nothing is a failure.

CQ: Totally. For me, success is based on one thing: being liked. Success isn't measured in square feet or in dollars, but in the mark you leave on other people. I always say that in life you have to work towards your funeral: you want it full of people who loved you in life and who will miss you. Why? Because if your wake is huge and the people who attend will truly mourn you, then you're immortal. You have a daughter and so do I – mine is younger – and what I want is for her to look around on the day of my funeral and say: "Damn, people loved my dad." And for someone to say to her: "Your dad was a noble man, and a good person. We'll miss him." That is being immortal. You can leave your kids a lot of things, but no legacy could be greater than that. For the years to go by and people to still talk about your father because he's still in their hearts, even after he's physically gone.

CK: Did your business failures affect your family life?

CQ: Sure. I don't have a family life, or a private one, or a personal one, a work one; nothing. All of my life is the same one. I don't get home and leave my brain at the door. Everything is continual; all mixed together. I could be at an event and think about my daughter, or my wife, or my mother, or my sister, or my team, or my friends… Or I could be with a friend and think about Valor de Ley or about the restaurants or business owners I advise in their personal and professional positioning – that is, doing what I call people SEO, so they can meet other people of interest to their lives and businesses. Everything is linked.

CK: Would you do anything differently from what you've done?

CQ: Yeah, sure, because you learn as you go. If you and I talked in a few days' time, maybe I would think something different, because I'm always open to change if someone convinces me I'm wrong. I'm not interested in people who say: "These are my principles and I'm sticking to them." I'm also not interested in people who can't laugh at themselves.

CK: I completely agree. Laughing at yourself is one of the healthiest things you can do. And it helps you progress as a person; helps you grow. For example, I laugh at my accent a lot, at my foreigner's appearance. Sometimes people ask me where I'm from, and I answer "Me? I'm from right here in Spain." And we have a laugh about it.

We have been chatting for almost three hours, and I know Cipri has a lot of commitments, so I don't want to take up any more of his time. I ask him my last few questions:

CK: Looking back, is there anything you regret?

CQ: Yes: the things I haven't done, of which there are many.

CK: Do you have a bucket list?

CQ: I used to write things down, but then I'd forget I had written them down. So I just decided to live day-to-day and not set myself goals. I begin each day by thinking: "What are you going to do to make today special? Who can you help?" Because of all the things I have left to do, the most important one is to leave a legacy of love. That's what motivates me every morning when I get up. My strategic plan starts again each morning, because every day is unique and it enables me to learn and grow.

CK: To finish with, what would you say to somebody who's screwed right now and is about to topple off a cliff, or even someone who already fell and doesn't know how to get back up?

CQ: I'd say: if you're in a hole, it's because you didn't follow your heart – you didn't do what your soul was telling you to do. If you want to get back up, do what your heart says – it will never steer you wrong. Even if you fail at a business, or at a hundred of them, you'll be happy, because you did what you wanted. And if you get back up to the top, you'll be equally happy, because you stuck to what you always wanted to be, to your spirit and your heart. What success is, really, is failing and still being surrounded by the same people:

your family, your partners… My success is the success of those around me. That's it.

CK: Totally.

I say goodbye to Cipri feeling that his words have been golden to me. A real treasure and a gift: pure creative, loving energy.

"

Cipri Quintas:
Nobility and honor
above all, even above
financial profit. I want
to walk with people who
are walking alongside
me, no in front, because
they'll block my way and
I won't be able to see
where I'm going.

"

JACK VINCENT (1957)

18th May 2020.

One day, a little over three years ago, I got a message on Twitter. Back then, I was pretty active on the social network and posting a lot of things about starting up businesses. I looked at the sender and it was Jack Vincent. He told me he found my posts interesting, and suggested meeting up for a coffee, since we were both in Madrid at the time.

I already knew Jack through social media. I had been following him for a while and was very interested in his focus on storytelling in sales, so I was flattered by his message and proposal.

We met in the neighborhood of Malasaña, where he has a house. We were talking for over an hour, and really clicked. We talked about endless things, but above all about starting businesses.

We've remained in contact ever since and kept up an online friendship. It's rare that we're in the same place at the same time, given that he lives in Lucerne in Switzerland and I'm always on the move, hopping from country to country.

A few months ago, before the quarantine, we were both back in Madrid and took the opportunity to meet up. It wasn't long before this damn lockdown started. Now, we have to make do with Zoom, just like half of Spain and the rest of the world are doing.

Jack comes on screen in what appears to be his office; behind him, I see bookshelves and a full video recording kit, with a tripod, spotlight, diffusing screen, and even a microphone that looks straight out of a recording studio.

He looks good. Despite being over sixty and having almost totally white hair and beard, he still has a youthful air about him. Under his black plastic-framed glasses, his eyes sparkle every time he talks about an idea, and his mouth widens in a contagious smile, as if he were about to tell a joke and is already laughing about it.

After we say hello to each other, I describe the book project in detail, since we've only exchanged a couple of messages on the subject. We speak in Spanish, with the occasional involuntary slip into English.

JV: I think it's a great idea to talk about failures and how to get past them. In fact, I've been to one of those annual conferences where people talk about their failures; I've even taken part, when I was asked to. But I don't think it's something to talk about with pride. We shouldn't forget that our aim is to do business and be successful at it. If we fail, we should learn, but not be proud of it. I mean, you can be proud of having tried, but not of having failed.

CK: I completely agree. Some people relish failure,

and talk about it as if it were a triumph. And it's not. If you have to fail, fail – there's nothing wrong with that. There is something wrong with failing and not learning from it. And worst of all is failing twice for the same reason...

JV: That's it.

CK: For those who don't know you, tell us briefly who Jack Vincent is...

JV: I'm the founder and managing partner of focus360, as well as the creator of my own sales method, S.C.O.R.E ©. My first love, though, was writing. I went to university in Syracuse, one of the best journalism schools, and I graduated as a magazine editor. My specialty was writing and editing magazines. When I was at college, I studied for a year abroad, in London. I had a great time. I took the chance to visit Barcelona, where I met the woman who would later become my wife. Two years after I finished college, I went to live in Barcelona. I couldn't find work as a journalist, so I got into the media, marketing and then sales. And it started to go well for me. I got to be head of sales and marketing at Ralston-Purina, and I launched some breakfast cereals that had a market share of 6% within six months. I had a future there, because the next step would have been to expand into southern Europe, but a headhunter made me an offer I couldn't refuse: working on a project related to the Barcelona '92 Olympic Games. It was 1989 and the whole city was pulsing in anticipation for the Games. There was a real buzz in the air. I loved the idea of being a part of it, so I accepted the offer, which consisted of working for an agency of the International Olympic Committee, ISL Worldwide. I was in charge of putting sponsors in touch with the Games. There were big multinationals like Coca-Cola, Visa, Panasonic, and so on. My job was to take care of relations with them, and manage the implementation of the Olympic sponsorship program. After the Games in Barcelona, I was transferred to Atlanta to head up the office there, but after a while we already had the sponsors and I was bored. It was a great job, because the money was good and I was well-respected, but I didn't have that drive. I tried to get the agency to take part in the 1999 Pan American Games, which were being held in Canada, but they weren't interested: "Too small for us", they said. So I decided I would do it myself. All I needed was someone to finance me. One day, when I was in conversations with the organizers, Frank Palmer called me: the CEO of a publicity agency in Canada called Palmer Jerry's, which would later become DDB Canada and then OMNICOM Canada. Frank was prepared to take the risk and finance the project. He knew about communications and he had contacts in Canada, while I knew about how to sell sponsorship programs, including TV rights. We created a company and agreed on a fifty per cent split of the profits. He put the money in – a million dollars – and I put in the hard work. It was the first time I had set up on my own and stopped being an employee on a payroll. What an opportunity! And what a responsibility…The plan was not to make any profit the first year, recoup our investment by the end of the second, and, all being well, get a lot of profit the third and fourth years. But by the end of the second we still hadn't closed the TV deal, and we had run out of money. Frank, who believed in me, put in another million dollars – but he was nervous. It was a risk, as our competition had convinced the game organizers that they could get more money from TV than us. We had a lot of interest from sponsors, but they wouldn't sign unless we could get a good deal with Canadian TV. It's a long story which I won't bore you with, but after numerous difficulties, and on the verge of losing all our options, we managed to unlock the TV issue and we signed great contracts with around a dozen big sponsors, like IBM, Panasonic, Royal Bank of Canada, and so on. And the Pan American Games were the most successful ever, both from a sporting and a marketing point of view.

CK: How did that success make you feel?

JV: I realized that, essentially, what I had identified as a good business opportunity years before had indeed turned out to be one. I mean, I had had a good vision, found a good partner, hired a good team and been able to manage a great project successfully. So I was satisfied. Not just because of the money, but because of everything I'd learned. In the closing ceremony, I looked over at Frank, who was sitting on my left, and I realized that he had been more than just my partner: he'd been my mentor. We never said it, but in practice, that was how it had been. I learned a lot from him, and not just the things he told me but the things he asked me, too. Today, he's a legend in Canada; he's achieved some important things. He was president of OMNICOM Canada and a member of the board for the agency at a global level. We're still in touch, even though he lives in Vancouver and I'm in Lucerne. He's a great guy. I love him!

CK: What did you do after that?

JV: I made quite a lot of money from it, but I didn't know what to do next. There was the option to create my own sports marketing agency, but I was unsure. Sometimes I look back and regret not doing it. I'm not one of those people who says: "Non, je ne regrette rien". There have been times that I have regretted not starting my own agency, even though I'll never know how it would have gone. What I did instead was accept a great offer to go back to the Swiss agency I had worked for for four years previously. I moved to London and became the brand manager and headed up the ATP Tennis Masters Series. My wife didn't want to live in London with our kids, so she went back to Lucerne, and I would go visit them at weekends. As well as all that coming and going, I would travel every two weeks to a different tennis tournament. I always got VIP treatment. It was a time of constant travel. But twenty months later, the company was bankrupt. I could give three operative reasons why ISL went bust, but I'll just venture one: politics. Everyone was so eager to climb the ranks in the company that they stepped all over each other any time they got the chance. I got stepped on a couple of times, too, but all I wanted was to do my job well. Everyone was criticizing what everyone else was doing, but they weren't doing a thing to benefit the company. After it went bust, we were talking one day, and I said "I feel like I've failed." And they said, "No, it's not your fault, it's this person and that person's fault." And I replied, "No, it's mine. And it's yours, too. But don't worry; I'm not going to put it on you. I'm simply shouldering my portion of the blame."

I learned a lot from that situation. I learned that the world of sports is full of big names, but also full of mediocre sellers and mediocre leaders who only get by through political games.

CK: Would you say that was your biggest failure, or, as I like to put it, "non-success"?

JV: I'd say so. It's true that I could blame those mediocre leaders who wasted so much time on politics, but it's also true that I got too used to not taking any risks. I did my job and defended my projects, but I didn't get involved in the bosses' decisions. I could see they were on the wrong track, but I stayed in my lane. I was genuinely busy with my own work, but I could have spoken up and said, "Hey, this is fucked". But I didn't.

CK: How did you feel?

JV: It hurt a lot. I was coming off the back of a big success with the Pan American Games – a warranted success, because we had to overcome significant obstacles to get there. But with ISL we couldn't find a way to get past the obstacles. It's true that it was a more complex organization and that it wasn't all down to me, but I could see us heading for a cliff and I couldn't build a bridge that would stop us from falling. It was so frustrating. I regretted not having talked to my bosses before, to tell them what I had noticed and ask them to let me act on it. That would have earned me some enemies among my colleagues, but at least we would have been saved, I think. But I didn't. The company went under in May 2001 and we were out on the street.

CK: How did you get past it?

JV: Well, luckily I had some money saved up thanks

to the success of the Pan American Games in Canada, so I decided to take that summer just to rest and be with my family. In September, I was starting thinking about what to do — but then two planes crashed into the Twin Towers, and the world stopped turning. It was like it is now with the coronavirus, but in the space of two hours. And I fell into a depression. I didn't have many friends in Switzerland, and I was still emotionally getting over the closure of ISL. I realized that some of my colleagues were relocating to other sports marketing companies, especially the ones who worked in football, and some of them had set up a little agency. But I didn't find my niche there. No one wanted to hire me — especially people in the tennis industry. I got to the last stages of a few selection processes, but I didn't get hired. I felt rejected, and it hurt. It felt so unfair, since the failure of ISL hadn't been my fault, but I had this professional stain. I was trapped in that feeling of injustice!

CK: And what did you do to get out of it?

JV: I started studying religious history as an intellectual exercise, and I ended up really identifying with Buddhism and Taoism. I applied Buddha's teachings to my life, and came to a conclusion: "*Life is a bitch, anything else is a bonus*". That changed me. It came to me at just the right moment, because my heart was open to it. There's a proverb that says: "When the student is ready, the teacher will appear." So I started to appreciate the little things. Even my morning coffee was a "bonus". And it stopped being so important that somebody hired me to work in the sports marketing industry.

CK: And you started another business...

JV: Yes. In 2002 I founded focus360, a sales consulting firm. It's a company that helps all kinds of businesses sell more successfully. And I created S.C.O.R.E. ©, which is a modular sales method, adaptable to each kind of acquisition and focused on clients. Since then, I've worked with some amazing clients: IBM, Master-Card, Swatch, Ricola, NBC Universal, Celgene, KPMG, and others. I also work with startup accelerators. I love working with startups because they have this real hunger to improve their sales. But the most important thing is that I feel I add value, and I have fun. And I have time left over for my true passion, which, as I was saying before, is writing. Over the past twenty years, I've been able to write a lot. I've written three books and I'm currently on my fourth. I'm sixty-two and I no longer want to spend all day working, like I have done at other points in my life. I don't want to break my back. But I'm still active and have a lot of projects on.

CK: Have your successes and failures affected your personal life?

JV: I'm sure they have, though they weren't the reason for my divorces. My first wife was a Spanish woman I married in Barcelona, and my second wife was Swiss-Italian. I had no kids with the first, and two with the second. She came with me on my Canadian adventure, but when that finished in 1999, she decided to go back to Lucerne. We already had our eldest, who was seven, and she was pregnant with our second. And she wanted to have the baby in Switzerland. Then I spent two years coming and going, living in London, and we were okay, but things turned over time. Even then, we held on for seventeen years, before getting a divorce nine years ago. But we have a great relationship; we all have dinner together as a family most Sundays.

CK: What would you say to business owners having a hard time with the current crisis, or ones who have had to close their doors?

JV: There is no magic pill. I'd just tell them they're not alone; that so many people have been through this and come out on top. You don't stop being valuable because you have one failure, and they'll have more chances later to prove their worth. And I'd tell them that the key is to sell. They might need to review their sales strategies or methods. If you'll allow me this little plug, I'd advise them to read my second book, *A Sale Is a Love Affair. Seduce, Engage & Win Customers' Hearts.* And I'd also advise them to feed their curiosity, more than ever. Get involved in the community, contribute, help others who are having an even worse time. Because that makes you value what you have. There is always someone worse off than you. Finally, I'd tell them that if they're feeling down, don't set themselves very ambitious goals. Don't try to build Rome in a day. Do small things: that will help to boost their self-esteem and make them feel capable, and in time, they'll be able to aim for bigger things.

CK: What advice would you give someone who wants to start another business?

JV: I would tell them to hire carefully; empower their team and give them resources and responsibilities; try to get people to treat each other well, like, there can be criticism, but with respect; and let people go when you need to, when someone's a bad fit, but do it nicely. Good leadership is like being a good teacher:

it's not about giving orders, it's about giving each person the means to give the best they can. Figures and results are important, of course, but if you want to lead people, influence people, persuade people, then you need to focus on the human condition. Strategies and implementations are more effective when you have people at the center.

CK: Have your priorities or values changed since your professional failures or successes happened?

JV: I've changed. I've gone from being an extrovert to an introvert, or should I say "ambivert", since I have qualities from both. If all this coronavirus and quarantine stuff had caught me a few years back, I would have gone crazy – now, I'm loving it. I've got this book about love in the time of corona and I'm having a great time. I'm really motivated by creativity; I want to do creative stuff. I often stop myself when I'm driving or cooking or working out, to take notes on my phone, because those bright sparks you get in your mind are amazing opportunities to keep learning and creating. You have to capture them so they don't disappear. I also love having conversations like this one with you, because even though my creative content hits me when I'm alone, it always comes after interesting conversations. Ah – and another thing that's changed is my spiritual dimension, which has grown. Now it's clear to me that you can't seek happiness outside yourself. "Outside" is a space for sharing happiness with others. The true artist, creator, is less interested in impressing than in sharing. And in the end, that's what makes a good entrepreneur, too: creating and sharing.

CK: Perfect, Jack. I think that's an excellent end

note for this awesome interview.

I thank Jack for his time, and we end up talking – strangely – about poetry, something that doesn't seem to have much to do with business…Or does it? Someone who has business in their blood can turn poetry into economy, and economy into poetry. Jack is definitely that someone.

"

Jack Vincent: Figures
and results are
important, of course,
but if you want to lead
people, influence people,
persuade people, then
you need to focus on the
human condition.

MARC REKLAU (1973)

www.marcreklau.com
www.linkedin.com/in/marcreklau

20ᵗʰ May 2020.

Today is my interview with Marc Reklau. I've known Marc, a fellow German, for years now. The last time I saw him was a little over a year ago, at a mastermind about habits, productivity and entrepreneurship that we organized together and held on his boat, moored at the Premià de Mar port, near Barcelona. We were a small but highly-motivated group. Good memories – doesn't time fly?!

Marc, for those who don't know him, is a bestselling author, lecturer and expert in personal development. His aim is to provide people with the necessary resources and tools to build the life they want. His first book, *30 days: Change Your Habits, Change Your Life*, has been read by an incredible two hundred and fifty thousand people, and translated into over fifteen languages, including English, German, Korean, Japanese, Portuguese, Russian, Chinese, Indonesian, Thai and Italian, among others. In total, his books have reached over four hundred thousand readers. But that's been no coincidence; it was the result of two years of hard work learning how to be a successful Amazon seller. As a personal development consultant, he helps companies improve their working environment and culture to get more commitment from their employees, higher levels of retention, and, as such, lower staff turnover.

We connect via videocall, as we've all had to get used to doing lately. He's wearing a navy blue T-shirt emblazoned with *Just do it* across his chest. It's a slogan that fits his character perfectly: direct and determined. I'm still wearing my tracksuit (it's not hot in Madrid yet), this time a Timberland one in dark green.

Marc is on his boat, where he's been living for the past couple of years, though he plans to move soon. He's a nomad, like me. The first thing he tells me is that he's sick of the lockdown and that as soon as they open the borders, he's jumping on a plane and leaving. I can really tell from his gestures that he feels restless, although he's pretty much like that even under normal circumstances: a real fidget.

Before we start the interview, we rant for a good while about the quarantine and government decisions regarding the management of the pandemic and their inability to run the country properly. Not only are we as businessmen and freelancers being clobbered with taxes, but they change their minds one day to the next, so we can't even trust them. I guess that's why we've become nomads and we don't expect anything from the nanny state.

After getting that off our chests, I begin by asking Marc to tell me his story briefly, like I have done in the other interviews.

MR: Well, I'm the same as you; I don't really like to talk about myself. But I understand people will be curious to know the people behind the book, so I'll think of a few things to tell you... I was born in Germany, specifically in Esslingen amb Neckar, a city in the Stuttgart region. The first twenty years of my life were very normal: school, friends, football...Then I studied a course I didn't like, International Commerce, and I started work in a job I hated. I held on for ten years, until in late September 2003, when I was thirty, I got fired. That was the beginning of a new chapter in my life. I was faced with the choice of finding another job, or starting up on my own. Until then, I'd never felt any entrepreneurial spirit: I preferred safety, and I was a little fearful. I was afraid of failure and rejection, and that fear kept me stagnating, thinking "it's not really that bad like this". But in life, if you don't make decisions, others make them for you. It could be an accident or illness, or your boss could let you go, like what happened to me. I decided to set up a life coaching business. Luckily, I had some savings, I had trained as a life coach, and I could claim unemployment, so I had some time to prepare. In the six months that I was unemployed, I studied digital marketing and saw that it was important to have a book as part of my strategy. I wrote *30 Days* and released it on Amazon in August 2014. For a few months, nothing happened. I mean, it didn't sell. I kept looking for information and learning how to sell online, but it wasn't taking off. In January 2015, only eight copies sold. EIGHT! I just thought it wasn't going to work, and I thought about looking for a stable job. But something inside me said, "don't give up yet". Then I spied an opportunity. A newsletter, BookBub, proposed that I offer my book free to a million people interested in self-help, as that's my target market. It cost five hundred dollars, but I took the risk. Suddenly, within days, I had forty thousand free downloads of the book. And then, once the promotion was over and the book went back to its price of $2.99, I started selling between eighty and a hundred books a day. I was so happy! I thought I'd finally cracked it, and that I could live off writing life coaching books. But then something happened: I relaxed. It was weird: I'd always been so afraid of failure, but it had never occurred to me that success could be dangerous, too. Even more so than failure.

CK: That's very true.

MR: It is. There are thousands of books telling you how to be successful, but none of them warn you of the dangers of success. They don't tell you you need to be very careful of its side effects. In my case, success made my lazy and complacent. I let my guard down. In 2015, I was lucky enough to sell a lot of copies of *30 Days*, and in 2016 I was invited to several international conferences, but the following year I analyzed my finances and saw that I was spending more than I was earning – I was burning through my savings.

CK: It took you a while to notice, then?

MR: My problem was the same one many people have: when things start to go wrong, they bury their heads in the sand. In my case, what was going wrong was that I wasn't selling so many books any more. My sales were declining, and so was my income. And numbers never lie. So I started to feel like a failure again, and once again I thought about looking for a job. But I decided to try again, again. I analyzed my situation and saw that, even though I was sometimes hired to do life coaching or speak at conferences, what brought the most money in was the books. It was very unusual, because most life coaches earn very little from their books and mostly live off the coaching. But it wasn't that way for me. So I decided to look at some authors that earn a lot from their books. I discovered that there were some in the US who were earning twenty to thirty thousand dollars just from books. I bought a course from one of them and it cost me a thousand dollars, which I had to pay in instalments, and started applying the things it taught me. It was more or less what I was already doing, but with a few important differences: that author had a lot of books, and invested a lot in advertising. And it worked. In just three months, I recouped my investment in the course and started making money. That's something I've done several times and I recommend it to entrepreneurs: even if you don't have much money, invest it in training. Look at what the big players are doing and educate yourself with them. In my case, it wasn't just profitable, it was super-profitable: in two years, I multiplied my book sales twenty, twenty-five times.

CK: How have you felt about failure throughout your life?

MR: Failure has been a loyal companion to me for much of my life. Fear, too: especially fear of rejection. But when I changed my relationship with failure, I started to triumph. I began to accept that I had to fail several times before I could success one time.

And from that moment on, failure stopped hurting – at least, it hurt less than before. I mean, if you know and accept that to success one time you must fail nine, those failures don't hurt so much. It's more than that: if I need to fail nine times in order to succeed once, I try to have those failures as quickly as possible.

CK: What have you learned from the experience of selling your books?

MR: That I can't relax. Now, I constantly review my lists of sales and my campaigns to see what's working and what's not at all times. Plus, since I know self-discipline is a weakness for me, I'm more aware that I can't slack off and can't get sidetracked. On the other hand, I'm very careful with the perils of success. When you get up and you know you don't have to do anything urgently – that what you earn from sales that day will cover everything and give you something to save on top – it's easy to just not work. But that's a trap, because if you don't keep working, it'll all go down again. That's why it's important to keep working ten hours every day, whether you're successful or not. I don't always manage that, but I'm getting more and more disciplined with myself. I remember that one of the first things I heard from you was about that: you said you had to be a hard worker to be successful. Then I saw it in a lot of fields, such as in sports. Michael Jordan didn't get to be the best by chance: he was always the first one to bound out onto the court and the last one to leave. Lots of other sportspeople, too.

CK: Do you think your failures have helped you learn to avoid failure in the future?

MR: I've learned to avoid some, but life is a roll-

"

Marc Reklau: There are thousands of books telling you how to be successful, but none of them warn you of the dangers of success. They don't tell you you need to be very careful of its side effects.

"

ercoaster with constant ups and downs, so I have no doubt I'll make a mistake again somewhere and fall down. But I'm getting better at being prepared for that, and I know how to get back up after I fall. That's why I'm open to whatever happens.

CK: Are you still afraid of rejection?

MR: Yes, but I deal with it better. From time to time, for example, someone criticizes me on social media, or leaves a negative review on one of my books. But now that I sell a lot, I care less. I've learned that successful people always have a few haters.

CK: You mentioned you didn't like the course you were studying, International Commerce, but in a way that's what you're doing, isn't it?

MR: Yeah, but now I do it on my own and with my books. It's true that, although I didn't enjoy doing it, that course helped get me where I am today. Because within international commerce I learned business administration and languages, which helps me, among other things, to translate my books into other languages and to communicate with Spanish providers, American ones, and so on. The irony is that not only am I now making use of that knowledge in order to sell my books all over the world, but for the ten years I worked before going solo, I worked at a publishing house! Thousands of book covers ended up on my desk every month, which probably also helped me when creating my own book covers and knowing how they work. So my conclusion is that ultimately, everything you do in life will help you sooner or later. Even a course I hated and I job I didn't like gave me tools that have helped me to be successful today. That just reaffirms my belief that in every failure hides a learning opportunity. The key is to find it and keep going.

CK: Did you ever imagine you would get to where you are now?

MR: I've always been a dreamer, but – like I said before – my weakness was that I didn't make enough of an effort. I mean, I would dream, but without doing anything to make my dreams come true. And with the books, it's kind of happened the opposite way: I never dreamed of being a bestselling author, but I worked like a dog for five years, and now I am. In conclusion, no dream is going to come true without work, but by working hard you can make things happen that you never dared to dream. It's true that visualizing your aims helps, but the important thing is to keep moving forward, step by step, battling through hard times, and getting back up when you fall. I was on the verge of going broke and throwing the towel in two or three times, but I didn't. And in the end I got my reward.

CK: What would you say has been the key, apart from perseverance and hard work?

MR: I have held a belief since the beginning of my adventure: I have to do things differently from other people. When I got into life coaching, everyone was focused on assessing people and companies, and thought that selling books was a side gig. I tried it that way at the start, but I found success when I flipped it around and focused on the thing other people saw as secondary: selling books. I left everything else aside and concentrated on being the best at selling my books. That's why I sought out people who sold a lot of books, and learned their methods.

Marc speaks emphatically, with big arm movements and passion in his voice. Although his appearance – like mine – is that of the typical German foreigner, the passion with which he speaks has more of that Southern European warmth than it does that typical German distance. I'm the same. It must be the years we've both spent in Spain.

Every now and again, he opens his eyes wide, as if his own words were surprising him. Then he gives a mischievous smile, like a naughty child. I'm glad I can count him among my friends and that we can chat openly.

CK: When things weren't going as well as they are now, did you blame anyone? Or did you feel responsible?

MR: I've never blamed other people. If you do that, you're lost, because if it's other people's fault then what can you do? Who's going to resolve it? I shoulder my mistakes and my decisions, but with no guilt and without punishing myself – it's simply part of the process. One line of reasoning I really like is to think that in any one moment, I'm making the best possible decision with the information I have available in that moment. It's too easy to think that you could have made another decision in hindsight, when you have different information. But that kind of thinking is harmful and useless. What's important is to take note of your mistake, and not repeat it. If you don't learn from it, you'll make it again and again. And that doesn't just apply to business, but to other areas, like relationships.

CK: What do you do to recover from a mistake or failure?

MR: The turning point is always reflection. I analyze what I did well and what I did badly, and I correct it. Often, that's enough, because a failure doesn't necessarily invalidate everything you've done. Some things might still be valid, and others may simply need to be modified to get things working again.

CK: Do you ask for help in times like that?

MR: Yeah, I'm fine with asking for help when I need it. My mother, for instance, has always helped me a lot. And at first, my best friends supported me, too. Then I came to Spain and I didn't have a contact network, so I had to set about creating one gradually. But in the end, you're the one who has to come out on top, somehow.

CK: What did you feel in those difficult moments?

MR: Oof, lots of things: panic, anger, envy, grief – sometimes, joy. The good thing is that I allow myself to have those feelings. Happiness doesn't mean being cheerful all the time; it means embracing whatever emotional state is occurring at any one time. All our emotions are trying to tell us something, so we have to listen to them and turn them into something positive. For example, I used to be jealous of authors who were successful with their books – until I learned to turn that feeling into admiration. And once I did, I started to look closely at what they did. Frustration, for example, tells us that we have the potential to do things we're not doing to the full. If we turn that feeling into a reflection rather than just holding onto it, we can find a way to let that potential grow. Emotions always have a reason behind them, and something valuable to teach us. For example, sometimes when things are going badly, I feel sad. It's like a kind of minor grief. And

I have several options: I can think about the things I'm thankful for or go for a half-hour walk till the feeling passes. But maybe what I want to do is just spend a day on the couch, feeling that sadness, observing it and finding out what it's trying to tell me. As you grow, you get to know yourself better.

CK: What would be your piece of wisdom regarding success and failure?

MR: That you can't give up. Like I was telling you, I've been a hair's breadth away from giving up a few times, but I've always found an inner strength that pushed me to keep going. And thanks to that, I've become one of the biggest-selling self-help authors in the world. In hard times, I remember a well-known phrase, which I bet you'll love, too: "When you feel like you can't do it any more, do it one more time." This is just a theory of mine, but I sometimes feel that the harder something is, the closer I am to my goal. Another thing I've learned, as I mentioned before, is that you have to work hard. Luck might work in the odd case, but 99.9% of successful people got where they are through effort and hard work. Finally, I've learned that the concepts of success and failure are in our heads. Who decides what's successful and what isn't? We all have our own ideas of success. It's a very personal thing.

CK: Looking back, would you change anything about your life if you could?

MR: The truth is that I wouldn't, because I believe that everything I've done and everything that's happened to me – including my mistakes – has got me here. I don't even have any hard feelings towards my old bosses, the ones I'm still in touch with and the ones

I'm grateful to for indirectly helping me achieve what I have done. They gave me the push I needed to take the leap. Now, it all makes sense – including the way I used to be, when I was a fearful person who clung to security. The only thing I regret is not having been nicer or fairer with people at times. But that's been useful to me, too, for having a better relationship with myself – the same way my divorce helped me have a better relationship with my current partner, Natalia. So, no – I wouldn't change anything, because if I did, my life wouldn't be what it is now. And I like my life.

CK: Have your priorities changed over time?

MR: I still like the same things; the difference is that before I couldn't do them, and now I can. For example, I love to travel, but when I was working at the publishing house, I could only do that during the four weeks of leave I got a year. Now I can do it whenever I want. Last January, for example, I went to Florida with Natalia. She's an entrepreneur like me, and we both worked in the mornings on our laptops at the hotel, and then for the rest of the day, we were just on vacation. I love that freedom. It's wonderful. I wouldn't change it for anything. It's my big raison d'être.

CK: I'm with you on that one hundred per cent.

MR: Yeah. And I don't just mean the freedom to organize my time how I want, but I mean financial freedom, too. That is, not having to worry about money, just take care of it.

CK: What would you say to someone having a hard time with the current crisis?

MR: I'd like to send them a positive message: that no matter what happens, it will all work out if they do what they can. It might not work out exactly how they wanted, but if they put their backs into it and learn from their mistakes, and if they push through any fears they have, they'll get somewhere good. And I would also say, practice gratitude despite your challenges. To begin with, you're alive and breathing – thousands of people can't say the same due to the coronavirus. Gratitude is one of the most powerful forces in the universe. And it helps you to reprogram your brain to see the good things in life: the things you can't see when you're in negative mode. It helps you to see opportunities, too. And if you can see them, you can seize some of them.

We end the interview on this optimistic note. I have loved chatting with Marc, and I thank him for his honesty and his motivational message.

CK: See you soon, Marc.

MR: I hope it'll be over a good ham and some beers.

CK: Of course!

"

Marc Reklau: It's true that visualizing your aims helps, but the important thing is to keep moving forward, step by step, battling through hard times, and getting back up when you fall.

"

JAIME CHICHERI (1979)

www.jaimechicheri.com
www.linkedin.com/in/jaimechicheri

22nd May 2020.

Today I have my interview with Jaime Chicheri, founding partner of three online marketing agencies (Marketing Surfers, Engage WorldWide and Social Clubbers), spread over Spain and Latin America. He is also the creator of de Revenue Knowmads. Of all the list of potential interviewees I made a few days ago, Jaime Chicheri is the one I know the least, and whom I've done the least business with. That's why the first thing I do is ask him to tell me about his background and how he became one of the biggest online marketing experts in Spain and Latin America.

JCh: I was born in Madrid into a well-off family. My father was a partner at a small law firm that ended up becoming Ernst & Young, although I didn't find that out until three or four years ago, when he wrote his memoirs. He was always very private about his professional history, and I thought he had just been a worker who had become a director after a very long time. I'm telling you this so you know my story isn't one of those rags-to-riches ones. I had it easy from the start. My parents gave me so much that it was one of the very things that almost drove me to failure. When I was young, I was very shy. When I had to talk to adults, I would do it through a stuffed donkey called Kiko – an important character in my life. Once, my parents and I went on a road trip, and we had already gone over a hundred miles when they realized we had left Kiko behind. We went back, because they knew it was going to be a difficult trip without him. I had him till I was ten, when I lost him while moving house. Now, I have him tattooed on me, so I can never lose him again.

[He shows me the tattoo over Zoom. And yep, there is Kiko's head.]

JCh: My parents were lovers of windsurfing and going on trips. When they went traveling, they would leave me with Ade, a Portuguese lady who has passed now. She was like a second mother to me. There are barely any photos in my house, but I have some of Ade that I look at every day. She was very devout and she taught me her values. My mother, on the other hand, taught us other religions, like Buddhism and Hinduism. All of that means spirituality was very important to me; not in the sense of rituals, but in my beliefs. At first, I went to a school full of artists – the *Virgen de Europa* – where I was very happy, but my parents moved me to an Opus Dei school, where I got my high school diploma and college foundation course. The first day, my mother made it clear to them that I was there for an education, but that I had a papal bull…I had a bad time there. I didn't fit in. My friends would talk about estates, money and surnames, and I couldn't follow. I liked other things. Those years I spent feeling that I didn't belong really damaged my self-esteem. Then I started college, and I met the person who is now my best friend: a really great guy. We started out doing Law, but I would go to class and not understand anything. At first I took notes, but then I even stopped doing that. I just played cards with my friends. My mother was surprised that I wasn't mentioning my grades, asked me: "Jaime, how are your grades?" I said, "I don't know, they mail them home." "What, a public university and they mail your grades home?" She didn't believe me and she followed me to college. She looked at all the lists of grades, and when she got to my name, they all said the same: AFC. She said, "I hope that doesn't mean 'Absolutely no Fucking Clue'." It actually stood for "Absent From Class". Man, was she pissed…

CK: Haha, I'm not surprised…

JCh: Once she got over it, she asked me what I wanted to study. I told her marketing or psychology, but she advised me to pick Hotel Management. There were two good schools: one in Marbella, and the other in Santiago de Compostela. I enrolled in the latter, thinking there would be fewer distractions there. Huge mistake: it turned out that from Wednesday to Sunday, Santiago was taken over by partygoers. I fell in with a bad crowd again. At twenty I tried my first cigarette, got hooked, and started on weed. I've never abused drugs, but I did start to mess around, especially with cigarettes and weed, which I found hard to give up. I've spent too many years of my life wrapped up in that substance — not doing sports, not going out with my friends because I preferred to stay home and smoke. It limited me a lot; but I don't regret it, because if I hadn't had that experience I wouldn't be doing the things I am doing, including helping young people to quit it... Anyway, I spent the first year partying it up and I failed three subjects. I couldn't pass the year. My mom told me, "If you fail this year, your future is going to be working as a waiter, dawn till dusk, with no prospects. By yourself." It was a wake-up call for me and I got my ass into gear. From then on, I started getting good grades. People were copying my notes, because my mom had taught me how to make mindmaps to make studying easier. Then I realized I wasn't bad at studying, I just hadn't found the right method or a subject that interested me. It wasn't till many years later that I discovered I had ADHD. I found out because my wife's middle child has it, so I read a book about it and I suddenly said: "Shit, this is me." Before then, people didn't know about it, or it wasn't talked about. People just thought you were stupid. You thought it about yourself, too.

CK: And when did you decide to set up on your own?

JCh: The first time I thought about it was at Hotel Management school. Antonio Catalán came to do a talk, and he told us how he invented NH and then AC (hotel chains) and I thought: "This entrepreneur thing is pretty cool." But I thought it was something for other people, not for me. Then I had a couple of ideas, like making T-shirts with the lettering velcroed on, but they already existed. I also had the idea of creating a vending machine with whiskey and ice for nightclubs, but nobody liked it. The craziest idea I had was an inflatable toy for dogs, because I had one, El Chino, and I had to have him neutered. But that had already been invented, too. So I was just turning ideas over in my head, more of a hobby than anything else, but none stuck.

CK: Were you still working in the hotel industry?

JCh: Yes, until the crisis of 2008. I had a well-paid job, and suddenly one day they told me they weren't renewing my contract. Very shortly after that, my then-wife told me: "I don't know if I love you". And just like that, having always lived a charmed life, my job and my wife were gone. Over time, that turned out to be the start of the best life I could have wished for, but right then, I felt totally screwed. I could have gone back to live with my parents, but I was nearly thirty, so it wasn't the best option. And I started to think about what I could do. I had been writing a blog for a while and I was interested in the world of marketing. I met Juan Merodio through LinkedIn and things started to fall into place. I thought about setting up my own business. One day I met up with him in a café in Madrid and I suggested creating an online marketing agency. It was going to be called Hotel Marketing Revolution, but he had a lot of vision, and said it wasn't a good name. And so Marketing Surfers was born. Juan taught me a hard work ethic. He was and still is very hardworking. And from then on things went really well. I started creating other projects, like an influencer agency. I think it was the first in the world, because

I'm talking 2009, here. I also set up a training center, but that was a bust. Then, with Juan and Javier Sanz, we created elsecretode.es, where we would share our entrepreneurial secrets. And a book: *The Digital Marketing Bible* (not yet available in English). In Colombia, we started an agency with Isra García and Óscar Valdelvira, Engage WorldWide, which was kind of a failure because we didn't understand the local culture. Plus, the value of the local currency went down and it was impossible to get any money out of it, because the government was keeping fifty per cent of it. So I decided to focus on Spain.

CK: Would you say that was your main failure as an entrepreneur?

JCh: I haven't had any big failures because I've never had to invest a lot in my projects. For example, setting up the Hotel Marketing School cost me under a thousand euros, and I'm getting two thousand a month from it. The other reason I haven't had any big failures is because I've diversified. Every year, I invent something new. The latest thing is Revenue Knowmads, the coolest project I've set up. The idea of it is that I teach people to start up in the hospitality sector, and I've created a community around revenue management, one of the bases of hotel marketing, so that entrepreneurs in the industry can help each other out. It's getting a really good vibe...So I haven't had any major failures, just a few small ones. But I've learned from those, too. I think the biggest failure would be not to learn. I've made a lot of mistakes, but I've learned from all of them, so I don't regret anything I've done. Every time I fail, I think, "Well shit, am I going to learn from this or what." I'm crazy, but I'm also very cautious. Every time I have to do a deal, I plan it all out. I do a mindmap, like my mom taught me. Revenue Knowmads is the product of a mindmap like that. And I didn't even need to make a financial plan. I don't feel comfortable with numbers. From what I know of you, you do get on well with numbers, but not me. I mean, I've felt impostor syndrome so many times, because I got into the marketing industry with no fucking clue about marketing. Over the years, I've learned, but someone who argues every day with distributors and clients knows a hell of a lot more than I do. What I know about is life, about entrepreneurship, about getting out of your comfort zone. That's what I wanted to dedicate my life to; not analyzing data on demand trends. That stuff is a real pain in the ass to me. I feel uncomfortable in a world full of numbers. I'm good with strategy, though.

CK: Have businesses successes or failures affected your personal life?

JCh: Yes, because it's difficult to separate one thing from the other. I'm a hyperactive guy; I get up at five in the morning to get the most out of my day, and I don't stop. That helps me stay alert and creative – to get a lot done and have a lot of ideas. Because I'm half cerebral, on my dad's side, and half creative – artistic, even – which is from my mom's family. My head just never stops. I'm always inventing things. But that hyperactive part of me also gives me trouble, for example with stress, which has affected my personal relationships both at work and in my love life. And with food – my big Achilles' heel is my diet. I don't eat junk, but I do eat a lot. And I have a tendency to put on weight. I can make myself a paella and spend three days eating it. It's not tenable. That's my big problem. It's like an addiction. Most people with ADHD have a tendency to form addictions. For me, smoking joints was a way of switching my brain off. In fact, I haven't totally given them up. Twice a year, I get together with my best friends and we just have a break. We spend two days smoking, watching movies, and switching off. And then, I gradually switch back on. I've had a lot of problems because of being this way, even with my wife, and I have a psychologist who helps me – she's awesome – and has helped me to grow emotionally.

What Jaime tells me about his ADHD really strikes a chord with me. I have been, and still am, a hyperactive person who doesn't stop dreaming up new projects. And at times, that has created relationship and communication problems for me. I would say I fit the profile of someone with ADHD ninety-nine per cent. So I hit pause on the interview for a moment to ask Jaime for his psychologist's details. He says her name is Sonia I decide to call her tomorrow, without fail.

We carry on:

CK: Now that you've mentioned emotions, how have your failures made you feel - angry, panicked...?

JCh: I'm actually very optimistic. I inherited that from my dad. So, every day I get up and set myself challenges. And my one big problem, which I'm trying to control, is food. I set objectives, but there's always a day that I fall off the wagon, and then it's just continued failure. But I even see that as something positive, because my life is so easy that I'm happy to have that ongoing battle. If I didn't have any challenges, and something to fight for every day, I might lose my lust for life. When it comes to emotions, I've evolved. As a kid I was always fighting with my parents over my grades. Then, I replicated that model in my professional and love life. When I started out as an entrepreneur, I had a team of fifteen people, and I allowed myself the luxury of yelling at them. Until one day, when I suddenly thought: "Who the fuck are you to go yelling at people?" And I forced myself to call the people I had fallen out with, fired or made things difficult for, and say sorry to them. Over time, I've learned – because I didn't know at the start. I was terrible at managing people, especially in stressful conditions.

CK: And now?

JCh: Now, I speak energetically, passionately, because that's my nature – but no yelling. I've learned to contain my anger, I've put strategies in place for doing that, such as meditation. I did a Vipassana retreat, which involves meditating for ten hours a day for ten days, in silence, and that helped me understand all those feelings. Now I know how important it is to be aware. And when you lose it, try to pull yourself together as quickly as you can. There have been times when I've felt panicked, too, such as when I got fired and my wife left me. And there have been times when I've been on the verge of death: when I got swept up in a current in the sea, when I took some ecstasy pills that didn't agree with me, when the car I was in fell into a ravine and the friend I was with died…But on a business level, no. I've always been lucky in business. Although, of course, if everything were to fall apart now, I would panic.

CK: You mentioned before that you were shy as a child. How did you conquer your shyness?

JCh: I was shy around adults, but with kids my age I was a bit of a clown. When I started filming training videos online, at first I was a little embarrassed to, but then I brought out that class clown side of me and people thought it was cool. So that encouraged me more. I filmed some more informal videos, and people said: "I liked getting to know you a little better". So I thought, "this is my thing". And I started with the bracelets, the bandannas. I am me, and I love it. Suits and ties aren't my thing. When we set up the agency, I said to Juan: "We need to give it a name people will hear and not expect us to be wearing a suit and tie." And so Marketing Surfers came about. I always just wear a T-shirt and come as I am.

CK: What motivates you most about the projects you start up?

JCh: I'm more and more motivated to help people. My wife and I take part in a lot of charity projects, like planting trees, sleepouts, things like that. I used to be embarrassed to say so because I didn't want to sound like I was bragging, but now, every time I do aid work I shout it from the rooftops, because it might get someone's interest. I don't care if people think I'm doing it to show off. In 2019, we swam across the Strait of Gibraltar for charity, and we raised thirteen thousand euros for children with leukemia. It was something that didn't resonate with me at first, even though I had had relatives with cancer. But it was the most beautiful thing I've ever done. I think that when you help someone who doesn't resonate with you, that's when you're truly helping. It was on this charity venture that I met Cipri Quintas, who's at the center of everything. He's everybody's friends. He's even got friends down in hell!

CK: Have your priorities in life changed since your experience as an entrepreneur?

JCh: A lot. For the first few years, my priority was to make money. But it wasn't so much that I wanted to spend it as that I wanted to save up "just in case". Now, my priority is to help other people and the universe. It's not about having a lot of money or a lot of security, because you never know in business, but one thing is clear: money is no longer my priority.

CK: What would you say to someone having a hard time with their business?

JCh: I'd tell them to go slow. Baby steps. Do one thing each day that helps them improve. Success is in the little details. If you keep working consistently, things will work out in the end. But you have to stay on the alert and not get too comfortable.

CK: How do you feel about your life right now?

JCh: I'm satisfied that I've taken the helm in my professional life, and, more importantly, that I enjoy every day doing what I do. I've been lucky enough to be a part of training over two thousand students and coordinating the marketing strategies for more than one hundred and seventy projects, from multinationals to celebrities and promising startups. I have my own online business school for training hotel owners in e-commerce, revenue management and online marketing, as well as lots of other projects on the go. It's so much more than I could have dreamed of that day in 2008 that I lost my job and started thinking about setting up on my own. As my favorite hashtag goes, I #CouldntBeHappier!

"

Jaime Chicheri: Now, my priority is to help other people and the universe. It's not about having a lot of money or a lot of security, because you never know in business, but one thing is clear: money is no longer my priority.

"

MÓNICA MENDOZA (1974)

www.monicamendoza.com
www.linkedin.com/in/monicamendozacastillo

24th May 2020.

The next interview I had planned was with Julian Hosp, a super interesting guy: a world-class expert in Blockchain, ex-professional kitesurfer, serial entrepreneur and endless other things despite his youth: he's only thirty-four! But yesterday in the early hours, he WhatsApped me to say he was in the middle of two functions for his project CAKE and would probably be a little distracted, so we decided to postpone it.

Today is Sunday, but for freelancers and business owners, it's a working day like any other. I have my interview with Mónica Mendoza, one of the contacts Josep gave me so that I could include women in the book. I spoke with her, and got a really good vibe. And not just that; she's a good listener, too. So much so that when we begin the interview, I forget to ask her any questions, and start telling her about my life, my teenage years, being orphaned. After an hour of talking about myself, I remember that I asked for an interview so we could talk about Mónica. So, I ask her to tell me her story. She gets right into it, and I quickly find out her adolescence was even tougher than mine:

MM: I'm the oldest of three sisters. My father, who emigrated from Andalucía to Cataluña in the seventies in search of a better life, was an alcoholic who beat us. Back then, it was really common in the lower classes for men to go out to bars and get drunk. It was actually considered socially correct. Then they would get home and take it out on their families. The neighborhood we lived in was a ghetto on the outskirts of Barcelona, L'Hospitalet, where crime and drugs were rife. That's the environment I grew up in. We had no money, so when I was eighteen, I started working on commission at a door-to-door sales company. It was cold calling, which is the toughest gig. All kinds of stuff happened to me: a man tried to rape me, my watch got stolen, a woman with Diogenes syndrome locked me in with several cats – and I'm allergic to cats. It took the police three hours to come and rescue me and get me to hospital, where they got me on cortisone and an oxygen mask. After that, I moved to a call center to do sales, and I saw older women there working on sex hotline, moaning while they crocheted or painted their nails. I don't know what the people who called those numbers were picturing, but the reality was far from erotic. I applied for a grant to study, but it got rejected. The thing was, my dad actually earned a decent amount of money – the problem was that he blew it all at the abr. One day, having had the shit beaten out of me, I told my mom I couldn't take it any more and that she needed to divorce him. We went to see a lawyer, we were there for an hour and got nowhere. But I realized we weren't going to be able to pay for it, so we had to just hold on. Those were some difficult years, always worrying about money. One day, I decided I wanted to study Psychology. I needed to understand why my father behaved the way he did; why he could be charming at times, and go crazy and aggressive at others. He actually had a personality disorder. I saved up, so excited to start my course, but I couldn't enroll because that year they raised the prices and I didn't have enough. I started crying right in the office with the enrolment papers in my hand, and the janitor, Zacarías, came to console me and give me a hug. The following year, I managed to enroll, and I graduated five years later. I remember one day, years later, I went into the college and said hi to Zacarías. "What are you doing here, didn't you graduate already?" "Yeah," I replied, "I'm here as a teacher". And he hugged me! Anyway, I'm telling you all this so you know I didn't have a normal childhood and adolescence. And there's a bunch more stuff, too, but I don't want to bore you.

CK: It's not boring at all, it's amazing.

MM: I've had an unusual life, with very emotionally intense experiences at a young age. And I'm sure my neural structures developed in a different way from most people's. I always had to overcome difficulties. For all the time I was studying, for example, I carried on working in sales or retail. Lessons started at three and I would get to college at seven. Do you know how I passed? Thanks to a blind classmate I had who would give me his notes in braille. I don't know braille, but there's software that translates it. Then I had to do the practicals, and since I was never in class, I got the ones no one else wanted: giving therapy to murderers and abusers in jail. As you can see, nothing in my life has been normal.

CK: When did you set up on your own?

MM: When I finished my studies I started working for Solostocks.com, from the Intercom group, as a saleswoman selling banners. I was good at it, and after a while they promoted me to Sales Manager. That's when I met Jordi, a super intelligent guy from Sarriá, a nice part of Barcelona, fell in love, and got married. I started to travel, to empower myself and to believe in myself. I saw another world. He supported me on my entrepreneurial journey; he made my business plan and encouraged me to create my sales courses. Seven years later, I fell out of love with it. I was making money with my training courses, but not enough to live on, so I had to juggle it with sales jobs – selling cardboard boxes and packaging. It's always difficult starting out, at least until you have a good customer base. I wasn't sure whether I should dive into creating my training company full-on, or look for something more secure. My mom told me: "Mónica, don't go self-employed, you won't have any money". So I did some tests as a university lecturer, and I passed. I lied to the dean and told him I knew about marketing. He asked me: "What do you prefer, strategic or operative marketing?". And I had no idea! I was a psychologist! At nights I would cram what I was going to teach the Economics students the next day. But anyway, I made a living and I ended up being the most valued lecturer there for three years. In the end, I quit, because my cachet as a sales coach was increasing and there was an opportunity cost there. And from then on, things just got better. Now I'm in the Top 100 speakers from Spain, according to Thinking Heads, and I give conferences and courses all over Spain and Latin America. And online, too, since the quarantine started. Oh, and I've published three books with Planeta: *What the Sales Books Don't Tell You*, *Motivation Pills for Salespeople and Entrepreneurs*, and *The Only 12 Ways to Get Clients* (not yet available in English).

CK: Not bad at all. Once you had started up on your own, what would you say was your worst moment?

MM: The hardest thing was getting divorced. I suddenly found myself working as a salesperson in the mornings and delivering courses in the afternoons just to get by and help my family. I would get home at eleven at night and still have to answer emails. I was sleeping five hours a day. Until I got hired by Renault to train people at their dealerships. Then I had another difficult moment: I set up a company with a snake oil salesman. He sweet-talked me with the promise I was going to become a successful woman. And being from the background I'm from, I thought: "This is my chance". But he turned out to be a scammer. He didn't do anything, and we still had to split the profits two ways. He even asked for a loan to buy a motorbike and a computer. I was quickly eating sandwiches between giving lessons and he was spending eighty euros on a meal. And on top of that, he tried to tell me I didn't have a businesswoman's mindset. Then I found out through other people that he was a con artist. In the end I sold him my share and I was fine, but I had a really bad time there.

CK: What would you say to someone having a hard time business-wise, like you were back then?

MM: To love themselves, to work on their self-esteem. Because when you feel weak, you're an easy target, and there will always be someone to take advantage of you. And then you feel even worse. It's a vicious cycle that will lead you to self-destruct. But it works in the other direction, too: when you empower yourself, you attract money and business, and that gives you confidence, so you attract even more money and business. You can't let other people look down on you, and to do that you have to start by loving yourself.

CK: What has been your biggest failure and how did it feel?

MM: My greatest failure was just not believing in myself at certain moments. That lack of trust in myself meant I put too much weight in other people's opinions instead of following my gut. It's not an easy thing to resolve, and to be honest, I'm still working on it, but it's so much better than a few years ago.

CK: Well you have no need to take others into account, your history of overcoming things is incredible. Is there anyone you blame for that "failure"?

MM: At first, I did. I thought it was my dad's fault, my family's, the neighborhood I grew up in, or just plain bad luck. I was in a spiral of blaming others. In the day I was cleaning at polo clubs, seeing the rich girls and thinking: "God, why me? Why am I always the messed up one, getting screwed over? Life is a pile of shit." Then one day, I stopped complaining, and said to myself: "Listen, Mónica, look at what you have – at your reality – what can you do to improve?". And I realized that there were a lot of things I could do. I realized that I could grab the reins of my life and that the only person responsible for my lack of confidence was me. Everything changes when you take control. You stop feeling like a victim of your destiny. It's easy to fall into feeling like a victim when things are going wrong, especially if you're an extremely sensitive person, like I am, who gets emotional very easily, even in business environments. I can't help it.

CK: I'm the same; I'm very sensitive. And I agree with you: if you dodge the issue, you get nowhere. If you think your success depends on your environment, you're on the wrong track.

MM: Yeah. But it's hard to learn that. The easiest thing is to feel like a victim.

CK: Was there a turning point when you decided to set up on your own?

MM: There were two key moments. The first was when I was still a salaried employee. A new manager came to the company who started mobbing me. She was a social psychopath. I had worked in prisons and I knew how to recognize psychopathy. That women started taking the credit for work I'd done, and threatening me, and it was then that I realized I didn't want to work for anyone. The other key moment was when I found out that a coach who had no idea what he was talking about had been paid two and a half grand – my monthly wage – for a one-hour talk. I thought, "If this guy with no experience, who only knows the theory, can charge that much, why can't I charge it when I've pounded the pavements and know a lot about sales?" I started giving courses at the offices of the company I was working for. I would bribe the concierge to let students in, and give courses to eight to ten people. People thought the offices were mine. And I was just bringing the concierge sausages and nice oil. I spent a year doing that.

CK: Has anyone helped you to overcome your obstacles?

MM: We all have angels who cross our paths. My blind friend from college, for instance, who I'm still good friends with. I was selling coupons in the mornings and studying Psychology at night. If it hadn't been for him, I would have failed my studies. Josep Lluís Llacuna, who introduced me to the college dean so I could become a lecturer, was another angel. He passed away, and I never got to thank him. Another was Jordi, my ex-husband, who helped to structure me a little and to love myself more. And he made me quit smoking, too. And Marcial, from Muebles 2000, who let me deliver a class in his store when no one was interested in them. There are lots of angels around; people who help us. It's rare that we stop to appreciate and thank them.

CK: What have you felt during hard times and how have you overcome those feelings?

MM: For a long time, I felt terrified that my dad would come home drunk. You never knew how it was going to be when he got home. When I heard his keys, my heart would pound…Then, when I was older, I would panic that I might run out of money. In fact, I still get that panic, I haven't gotten over him. And all my life I've felt angry toward people with money. I don't know why. I recognize that I get angry with people who inherit money or marry into it instead of earning it themselves. But, really, they have every right to, and feeling that way is something I need to work on.

CK: What have you learned from your rollercoaster of a life?

MM: One thing I've learned is that you need to take mental health seriously. Depression can be a very serious sickness. Another thing is that life can change from one day to the next, in a matter of minutes. Today you might be fine and tomorrow you could die. That's very powerful. And the last thing I've learned is not to complain. My mom taught me that one day. I came home tired having spent the day running all over the place, and after we ate, I put my son to bed and said to her: "Man, I'm exhausted, and I still have emails to answer." And she said to me: "Well, I'm happy; I cleaned the toilets and they told me I did a really good job." I had turned over two and a half thousand that day (not profit) and was complaining about my life, while she was happy because she'd done a good job cleaning. It was a real dose of humility. The problem is that we tend to naturalize successes fast, and stop valuing them. That's why it's important to appreciate what you achieve or have, even if it doesn't seem like much

CK: The lockdown has made me appreciate a lot of things. It's really reframed things for me. But it's true, sometimes we need to have some awareness of the fact that we live a lot better than the average person. Mónica, what would you never do again?

MM: Have a business partner. Maybe people think that's a bad mindset. But I don't care, I wouldn't have a partner again.

CK: Have your professional successes and failures affected you personally at all?

MM: Everything in life comes at a price. I've had to fight hard to climb the social ranks; that's not something you can do overnight. Now, I'm a sought-after speaker and a lot of people write to me, but this has its downside: I have no social life. I'm still working sixteen hours a day to maintain my lifestyle, which isn't even that extravagant. And I can't have a stable relationship because I travel constantly. Now, I've been going out with a guy for a year, but that's because he was already a friend and he adapts to me.

CK: But it's very impressive what you've achieved, considering your background and everything you've been through. It's enviable.

MM: I'm satisfied, because I've become pretty successful, but I also wish I could make more plans and have more of a social life. I've always lived from one day to the next, not setting myself any goals, and I end up not daring to say no to anything. My schedule fills up and I have no time for my personal life. I'd like to improve my quality of life; spend a little more time with my son, walk along the beach without worrying about the endless emails and messages I still have to reply to. That's why I'm exploring the idea of info-products now, and shifting my strategy towards digital. The Covid-19 crisis has given me the push I needed. It's been great for me.

CK: Have your priorities or values changed over the years?

MM: My values haven't changed. I've always had very clear ethical principles and have lived humbly: something I think is sorely needed. But since I became a mother, my priorities have changed. Now I wonder if it's really worth working such long hours. The problem is that, with what I do, you have to work a lot to make money, especially because the government keeps half – which I consider robbery.

CK: I completely agree. Do you have any regrets?

MM: Lots. I regret being so rebellious and giving my mom such a hard time, for example. I've never said sorry to her, because in my house we didn't show affection. We were too focused on just getting to the end of the month. We find it hard to show affection. We get together every Sunday, but I can't just look her in the eye and say: "love you".

CK: What would you say to someone in a difficult situation because of this crisis we're having; someone who's fallen down or is about to?

MM: I'd tell them to have perspective. This too shall pass. That's coming from me, who's been through all kinds. You have to put things in perspective. The sooner you let go of things, the sooner they stop hurting you.

I have loved chatting with Mónica. I didn't know her before, but now I feel like I've known her all my life. It occurs to me that we could do something to-gether, something bold: like get up on stage and tell an audience everything we've been through, her story and mine. I'm sure someone out here would say, "Well, my problems aren't so bad, I guess. Storm in a teacup."

"

Mónica Mendoza:
This too shall pass.
That's coming from me,
who's been through all
kinds. You have to put
things in perspective.
The sooner you let go
of things, the sooner
they stop hurting you.

UN BREAK

25th May 2020.

Today, Madrid moves into "Stage One", and I can finally move around a little: take my car to be washed, and find something to distract me after seventy days shut away and deprived of my freedom, the thing I value most.

I have really not liked the Spanish government forcing us to lock ourselves up (literally) for so long. This quarantine has been one of the worst experiences of my life. So much so, that I've decided that when we can travel again, I'm getting out of this country. I don't want the next outbreak to catch me in an apartment in Madrid.

Yesterday's interview with Mónica Mendoza was incredible: an absolutely amazing story. I went through shock, incredulity, rage, joy, and, above all, understanding. I'm sure it's going to be a very talked-about chapter!

The purpose of the book, as I was saying at the start, is for the testimonies of my interviewees to be of use to business owners having a hard time right now. However, I'm noticing a positive side effect: they're helping me to think about my own life, too. I see myself reflected in my interviewees, like a mirror throwing back things about myself that I hadn't seen or that I was ignoring. This was most notable when I talked with Jaime Chicheri. When he told me about his Attention Deficit Hyperactivity Disorder, it was like a lightbulb came on in my head. I identified so strongly with the symptoms he described: difficulty carrying out tasks that require concentration, lack of motivation when it comes to doing things that aren't stimulating, procrastination when I have to do repetitive tasks…

I've been turning it over for three days. I've read up on the subject and realized there's a lot of information about how this disorder affects children, but not a lot about its effect on adults. When I was little, people just said things like: "such a fidgety kid". If the information had been out there, I might have been aware I had a disorder and circumvented a ton of problems.

I've spoken to my daughter Jacquie about it. She's nineteen now. I think a lot of the problems we've had in terms of our relationship and communication might have their roots there. Because it happens so often that when people talk to me, I hear their words, but my mind is elsewhere. It's so hard for me to concentrate on things. For example, I find it hard to read books. I'll read a page, and then realize I don't know what I just read. Other times I speak without thinking; I'm too impulsive. This has helped me out of some difficult situations, but at the same time it's got me into a lot of disagreements.

My research has told me many of the main symptoms of ADHD relate to low dopamine levels. I bought some pills and started taking them a few days ago. I don't know if it's psychosomatic, but I felt great yesterday during my interview with Mónica. And today is the first day in a long time that I've been able to write without thinking about other things other than what I'm writing. In any case, I want to do things properly, so I've booked in to see the specialist Jaime recommended. I want a proper medical diagnosis and some strategies.

By the way, I don't have any interviews today, so I thought it was time to write down my own story in a little more detail. I'm German, and I came to Spain with my parents when I was eleven – specifically, to Tenerife. I didn't have a very normal adolescence. When I was twelve, my mother was diagnosed with breast cancer, and then began a long journey of hospitals, operations and chemo. My dad, who was thirty years older than my mother, developed a very severe and rapid form of Alzheimer's, and died when I was sixteen. My mother and I were left alone, but not for long. She tried hard to hide her pain and to educate me as best she could, but the illness consumed her little by little. She held on for as long as humanly possible, and after battling for six years, when she believed I was ready to go on without her, she let go in January of 1990.

And so I was left an orphan at eighteen. I did my final exams for the Abitur, the equivalent of Spain's university access tests, and passed with an average grade of "good". My mother had thought I would study at a Swiss hospitality school in Locarno, but I only lasted two months there. I missed Tenerife and my friends, who had become my family and my support network. I was an only child, and the few relatives and cousins I had were in Germany; I barely knew them.

I didn't want to keep studying, so I started work. For almost a decade, I worked at various companies – as I explained at the start of the book – but I was always attracted to the idea of setting up on my own. I was always inventing things; I had that restlessness. When I met the mother of my daughter, we set up a pet shop, and it went well. It really took off. Then I started the first business center in Tenerife, but I was too ahead of the game. People weren't ready. I'd seen them working in Madrid and I thought that since I was the first, it would go well, but sometimes it's better to be the third, like Cipri was saying the other day in his interview.

My toughest moment came shortly after that. I set up a construction and renovation company, I had a large non-payment, and I went under. I was ruined. I lost everything. Receivership, court appearances, darkness. We didn't have to sleep in the street, because my ex-mother-in-law had a house we could go and stay in. We had nothing. *Nothing.* Jacqui was two, and a friend of ours had to help us buy diapers. If I asked myself the same question I'm asking my interviewees, the answer would be: "*That* was my biggest failure. And yes, it was hard. Very hard." And what did I feel? Frustration, rage, powerlessness, grief…I'm a very sensitive person, and I cry easily, so you can imagine my reaction.

But I had a little girl, and I had to get through it somehow. I started selling life insurance. I studied how they do it in the US, their sales pitches, and it went pretty well. At least, I was bringing in enough to eat and pay bills. But I've always been restless, so even while I was selling insurance, I was thinking about doing other things: a restaurant, tree plantations in South American so I could sell would, and so on. Around 2004, a former supplier from the business center offered me some color printers to print the insurance quotes on. I told him I had no money, but he said it was no problem: "I'll give them to you on finance. Since we know you, if you come to the office once a month, give us some money and work your way through the instalments." That's when I learned that by facing things and doing things properly, you generate trust, which can open a lot of doors.

Anyway, because I had worked at a publishing house, I decided to start selling calling cards online. My offer was simple and cheap: a hundred cards in twenty-four hours for fifteen euros. Once I got an order, I would design the cards, show them the proof, print and ship. I set up a website and started getting orders from the mainland, too. So I started up Factoría Creativa, a company which still exists, though I changed it and now we make plastic cards like the ones issued by banks. We have branches in several countries, and now Eli, my left hand, runs it (my right hand is Lau, who I mentioned in my interview with Juan Merodio).

And that was the beginning of my comeback. After a year selling cards, I began to get customer requests for other products, since people saw I was offering good service, a good product, and I was doing what I said I would. That taught me the importance of keeping your word in order to create a good personal image. It also taught me the usefulness of contracting out in order to grow; for every order I received, I looked for the most suitable suppliers.

After that, I set up some more projects, some of them online, including an academy for helping entrepreneurs which I called CK Academy. After the failure of the construction company, where I had had around thirty employees, I was totally set on not having staff, and online businesses allow you to set up with very little investment and infrastructure. My problem is that I love to start new projects, but once they're in the air, I get bored (with the ADHD thing, I'm beginning to understand why), so I either abandoned most of these or gave them away.

I also quickly get bored of places, houses, environments. That's why I've moved around twenty-five times. I've lived in Germany, Spain, Poland, Greece, Romania, and now back in Spain, and I've spent short periods in other countries all over the world in between.

Nothing has happened in my love life, because I'm bad at flirting. I am totally useless at it. It's partly because I'm easily embarrassed and I feel ridiculous. Once I know someone, I don't get like that, but I find it difficult at first. And it's also because I'm afraid of failure. I think I was pretty traumatized by my big failure with the construction company.

In 2017, I started investing in bitcoins. It was before the boom, and I made a lot of money. Since I'm very open and I explain everything, some people asked me if I could help them out with trading. At first I was reluctant, because I didn't feel confident advising people, but then I decided I could just share what had worked for me. So I started a new business, Nomad Kapital (www.nomadkapital.com), which is a trust company (authorized to manage third party capital) registered in Sweden. I keep investors absolutely abreast of what I'm doing in a very transparent way, and so far I've ended every month in profit since I created the company. I don't want it to be something that grows a lot. I already have around a hundred investors and I set myself a limit of one hundred and fifty. That's a reasonable number to be able to stay in contact with all of them. In fact, I only accept people I personally know, or family and friends of existing investors.

So, my passions are entrepreneurship and investment. In both fields, I try to be consistent and generate trust. I do the same in every area of my life: I talk about what I'm doing and going through, not what others are doing. I don't copy-paste; I'm much more trial-error. I practice everything I preach, which gives me a lot of credibility. For example, I'm very critical about the State's role and about taxes, so I live in several countries in order not to belong to any single one. I have no fixed abode and I travel a lot. That works for me. I love to travel, to eat, and to talk, so I travel, I meet friends and clients, I talk to them (always with a good meal between us) and then I go on my way.

In terms of entrepreneurship, I find it fairly easy to have ideas and turn them into profitable businesses. I've done it twenty-two times in the past twenty years. I like it, and it's something that comes naturally to me. That said, over time, I've discovered that ideas alone aren't worth a dime; you have to execute them properly.

Without proper validation, the right business plan, and tailor-made financial projection, ideas are just short-term projects with little hope of success.

For a business to go well, at least four factors have to coincide, like legs on a table: the idea has to be good, the time has to be right, it has to be well executed, and luck has to be on your side, or at least, not so terrible. When one of these four legs fails, the table tilts. And if two fail, it crashes to the floor.

If your table falls and breaks, you might be tempted to blame other people. That's human nature. Over time, I've learned not to blame my failures on anyone. I always try to shoulder my portion of the responsibility. Things can always go wrong even if we work hard. That's just reality. For example, the government could take detrimental measures. That's why I understand the feeling of powerlessness that some entrepreneurs felt two and a half months ago, when they had to close their doors, not knowing if they would be able to re-open again. A virus appearing and the government declaring a state of emergency are not things we can control.

The stories I'm compiling in this book show that there is life after failure. Nothing is final and everything can be overcome except for death. And after failure, there is only one thing we can do: get up and start over (hence the book's title). Those of us with the entrepreneur gene don't give up, because we know that if we want to achieve our life goals, we need perseverance and attitude as well as intelligence, hard work and dedication. And above all, we need never to give up; you never know which one will be the one.

That's the most important thing about starting a business again: attitude, and enthusiasm. You don't need a lot of money. In fact, I founded all my businesses from nothing or with minimal investment. This is something that goes with my minimalist lifestyle. You'll always see me wearing the same clothes: T-shirts, joggers, possibly a shirt, and that's pretty much it. For a time, all I wore was white T-shirts from Primark. I went from there to white shirts – non-iron ones, to be specific. I wash them, hang them out, and they're ready to go. I don't like wasting time on unnecessary things. For me, the most important thing in life – the thing that brings me real satisfaction – is helping other people with their projects.

There has been a misconception doing the rounds in recent years, both among young people and not-so-young ones: find your passion and you can turn it into a million-dollar business. In my twenty years of experience, I've seen that it just doesn't work that way. Passion won't always find you clients prepared to pay what you want or need to charge. It's better to focus on projects with the potential to be profitable. Dedicate yourself to becoming the best in your sector, gain experience, and be appreciated and admired by your customers. Being passionate about doing your job well goes hand-in-hand with success.

Nowadays, looking back, I consider that the battles I've fought were worth fighting. I've done some good things – among them my daughter, who is nineteen at the time of writing. I like the fact that she questions things and thinks outside the box; she doesn't just blindly accept things. She has surprised us with ideas such as homeschooling until the end of her diploma, so that she can spend more time with her mother and me. Now, she's talking about studying for her future career online.

The most important thing is that everything I've experienced has taught me something new. I weigh things up and what comes to mind is that old phrase: "Sometimes you win…sometimes you learn". I think I've learned from all of it. And I feel that I've won, and that I keep on winning every day.

3rd June 2020.

As you can see from the date, it's been ten days since I did my last interview. The reason for this is that my dog, Kasia, who was diagnosed with cancer five months ago, took a turn for the worse. I haven't been in the mood to write; I've just been trying to spend time with her and be there for her. Today, I finally decided to take her to the vet to have her put to sleep. It was one of the hardest decisions I've ever had to make. I was with her till her last breath, and it was rough. I'm sad and exhausted. I really loved her, and I will miss her very much.

13th June 2020.

It's taken me ten days to get my head back in the game and pick up the book again. My grief over Kasia has been compounded by the discovery that I've suffered from ADHD my whole life and never knew it. And, of course, by the lockdown, which is gradually being relaxed in Madrid. I've been able to go out for walks and even to have a beer on a terrace somewhere for the past couple of days. It's still shocking to see Madrid half-empty. Here, the streets and terraces of bars and restaurants are packed with people nearly year-round, especially now, in late spring and early summer.

I don't want to leave this book unfinished – not just because I'm so excited about it, but because I think it's more and more necessary. There's more bad news about the economy every day. Some airline goes out of business every day and the stock market is stuck on a rollercoaster; some days shooting up, as if everything were going to be okay, and other days plummeting in response to a new outbreak in China or bad news about the pandemic's impact on the tourism industry. And I'm sure the worst is yet to come! The Spanish government has no other solution than to get into further debt (like it didn't have enough!) and it's going to take several generations to pay it off. This just confirms to me that I want to get out of here as soon as I can. Although, on the other hand, that makes me sad – I have a lot of friends here, and my daughter, and I want all of their futures to look a lot brighter than they are doing.

Within a few days, we'll be moving into Stage Three, and I'm taking my daughter to see her mom in Zaragoza. At least I'll be able to get out of Madrid and have a change of scenery. Meanwhile, I'll spend today contacting the rest of the business owners on my list and scheduling some more interviews. I'm really curious to hear how people are taking this crisis.

JUDIT CATALÁ (1986)

www.juditcatala.com
www.linkedin.com/in/juditcatala

17ᵗʰ June 2020.

After a weekend spent packing up the apartment in Madrid, I finally left town on Monday, the day before yesterday. I grabbed the essentials and came to Zaragoza with Jacqui, where she's visiting her mother and I'm taking the opportunity to take my car in for some repairs. I plan to go to Valencia from here for a brief stopover, and then on to Cáceres to pick up a camper-van I've bought so that I can travel freely throughout Europe over the coming months. I won't have a fixed house, but at least the next lockdown won't catch me stuck in an apartment in Madrid.

Today, I'm finally resuming my interviews. Today it's Judit Catalá, a young businesswoman I only know through social media so far. Josep put me in touch with her. They both live in Barcelona and know each other through another of my interviewees: Mónica Mendoza. It's a small world, as they say.

Judit comes to me from the world of marketing, and she's become something of a mentor in online marketing. She has her own training company for entrepreneurs. That is, not only is she an entrepreneur herself, but she helps others to make their businesses work via online and in-person courses. From what Josep has told me about her, she has overcome a real backstory of her own. I can't wait to hear from her – partly because, when we talked the other day to schedule our chat, she mentioned that she also had ADHD as a teenager. So, after the usual Zoom introductions, I ask her to tell me about herself:

JC: I had a very happy childhood. My parents met at a hikers' center, and all my early memories are of rambling in the mountains, cows in fields, gorgeous landscapes…A lot of happiness. My teenage years weren't so good. I wasn't a bad student, but I had ADHD and I found it really hard to pay attention. The teachers were always telling my parents: "She's bright, but the slightest thing distracts her". Even now I find it hard to concentrate and to focus on things. I can't sit still for long. If you made me sit in a chair all day, I'd just die. So that problem made my adolescence really hard. For a while I stopped going to classes. I had insomnia and by the morning I couldn't take it any more. The teachers would tell my parents that I wasn't making an effort, but the problem was that I just didn't see the point of it all. I didn't know what I wanted to do with my life, I didn't understand any of it, so I dropped out of high school. My mother told me I had to do something; that she wasn't going to let me sit around and do nothing. I come from a humble and very hardworking family. My dad worked at the port. He started out as an office worker and climbed the ranks till he had a really good position. He worked really hard, like me. And my mother sold clothes at a market. I started working with her and after a while, I decided to give studying another go. I enrolled in night classes. I would work, take a shower, and go to class. I met some amazing people there: people who were older than me and very critical of the education system, and we formed a kind of tribe. It was fantastic, because I suddenly felt understood. Then I went to college. I didn't get the grades for my first option, Psychology, so I went for Education. I juggled the market with my uncle's churro stand in Trinitat, a deprived area of Barcelona. I worked with him there on Wednesdays. At first, I was embarrassed, because it's a very populated neighborhood and everyone knows each other. And, of course, I was "Judit – the churro girl". My hair would smell of churros even after I'd washed it. But despite all that, I have fond memories of that time. I learned a lot of things, particularly, how to manage customers. You don't know how hard it is to deal with a line full of little old ladies, all pushing in!

CK: That's great!

JC: That's when I began to learn how difficult it is to sell things and run a business. Because a market stall or churro stand are businesses – they're modest ones, but they are still businesses. And you have to buy and sell and balance the register at the end of the day. And, of course, you have to understand what customers want. I've always been interested in the mental processes, the cognitive side. In fact, I work in marketing and sales because they're so closely linked to psychology. If you don't know how cognitive processes work, it's never going to go well for you. At twenty years old, I was already really tall, and I started getting modeling and hostessing jobs. I was earning quite a lot of money so I quit the churro stand.

I also dropped out of my course and started studying Publicity with Cataluña's online Open University. One day, working as a hostess at a food festival, I went to have breakfast with a customer from a winery and he asked me a question that changed my life: "Judit, who do you want to be? Where do you want to go in life?" Until that moment, I had never thought about it. I worked in the market with my mom, I went to auditions, I slotted in some modeling jobs, I did remote study…but I hadn't asked myself that fundamental question. So, for the first time, I did. And I realized I didn't want to be a pretty girl behind a counter. I wanted to start projects, do business. That's how I discovered that. It's crazy how a simple question can change your whole life, isn't it?

CK: Totally.

JC: I was in a relationship with a man a little older than me back then. He was a web developer, and I said to him: "Let's set up a company. I'll sell the websites and you develop them." And so it was at twenty-three, I founded my first company. Not long after that we rented a small office – tiny, barely two square meters – and we worked hard for four years to make the business work. I was still learning, and I realized that I liked digital marketing more all the time, so I did a masters and started doing SEO for a bunch of companies. But my relationship with my partner – romantic and business – was going from bad to worse. He couldn't stand the fact I was at the helm, and he made me look bad in meetings with clients. At home, he was getting more and more violent, and I started to feel scared. It didn't happen overnight. One day he got mad and started throwing things and yelling, but the next day he bought me flowers and was all sweetness and light. That's why so many women find it hard to realize they're victims of abuse: because these men can be so charming... But he was really rude to clients, too, telling them they didn't know what they were talking about. He would even yell at them. Some of them would call me later and be like, "God, I don't know how you can stand him." And others just left us. I was hung up on having my own business, because my life consisted of going round apologizing to people because he'd said something awful to them or treated them badly. It was terrible, I was just constantly crying. I don't think I've ever cried so much.

CK: Didn't your family tell you to leave him?

JC: My family didn't know, because he acted normal around them. Even the doorman on the complex where we had our office, on the Casp de Barcelona street, thought he was a nice guy. I remember one day, when we were having one of our fights, I said to him: "You don't realize what you're like; you don't even say hi to the doorman." And the next day he started saying hi to him and being friendly with him. He was a textbook sociopath, a total manipulator. My family thought he was awesome. But then he was so controlling with me. Now, I'd never tolerate that, but I was really young and I had to go through that to learn and become who I am now.

CK: Of course. We're the product of our experiences. If I hadn't gone broke and ended up penniless in the street, I wouldn't be who I am today.

JC: Sometimes you have to be with a manipulator to learn what manipulation is like and be able to detect it in the future. That's how we are. The problem was that when all that happened, I lost confidence in myself and in people. I'm naturally trusting and tend to establish trusting relationships, but in that situation, it was really difficult for me. It took me a long time to get over it, to let people be close to me again. In a way, I lost my innocence. Now, I'm still an open person, but if I sense that someone is lying to me, even in a small way, I quickly distance myself from that person. I trust everyone by default, I give everyone a chance and I let them in. But if someone lets me down, that's it for them.

CK: For me, everyone is good until proven otherwise. But when money is involved, I do a little more research on people. And I use social media. I used to just follow my gut, but it's let me down on occasion... Going back to your story, how did your relationship with your ex end?

JC: I held on for a few years, but it was torture. I ended up thinking that I was stupid and that I wasn't good enough to be in business. When I decided to leave him, I had a lot of doubts and didn't know what to do. In the end, it was thanks to a friend of mine who had had a similar experience. She said, "Judit, this isn't normal. When someone loves you, they don't treat you like this." I tried to break up with him several times, but I kept going back. One of those times was because my dad passed away; I was depressed and I needed some-one. So I called him.

CK: I understand. We're only human. My mother died with me at home when I was just a teenager. She was just over five foot and by the end she weighed sixty-two pounds, consumed by cancer. It's been thirty years, but the pain never really goes away.

JC: I adored my dad, and when I lost him, I needed someone to cling to emotionally. It was a moment of weakness. I went back to the guy and was with him for another year, until I felt overwhelming need to run. The threats and yelling were back, to the point that some of my friends were afraid to leave me on my own. Eventually, I decided to leave him. I was so scared that I left without taking anything; not a single euro. I didn't even have enough to buy myself a coffee. He carried on the business, and as revenge on me, he stopped paying taxes and the workers' social security. I spent a lot of time paying off debt. But the worst thing was the insecurity all of it left me with, because he had made me believe I was bad at business. I had to fight hard against my limiting thoughts, against my mental blocks. But I didn't throw in the towel. And now, seven years later, I'm bringing in millions.

CK: How did you manage to get past it?

JC. I carried that baggage for years, both financially and emotionally. I felt like such an idiot. I saw other people making bank, and there was me, working to pay off debts that weren't even mine. I would compare my-self to other people and come up short. That was until I decided to take control of my life, and I started doing research into what successful people did. Instead of envying them and feeling jealous, I started to admire and imitate them. Fortunately, I'm very hardworking, so I started following these people all the time – especially Americans – and training myself around them. And thanks to those mentors, I got out of the hole I was in.

CK: Did anyone in particular help you: a relative, a friend...?

JC: No, it was a process of introspection. Solitude helped me more than people did, because a more grown-up Judit could emerge, self-sufficient. I also didn't want to lean on my family, because I would have worried them. They must have known something was up, but I didn't tell them anything. I suffered in silence. I remember feeling very alone, crying alone, always being alone. I would share my fears with some people close to me, like my friend Veronica, who's an entrepreneur as well. But she moved to Mallorca and I had to get through it on my own. And I don't say that sadly, because it was actually a very positive thing. I would have liked to be among other entrepreneurs and share experiences with them, but it went how it went, and it really helped me learn a lot about myself.

CK: And what did you learn from it all?

JC: So many things. As a businesswoman, I learned to protect myself legally. Now, I always do. I never set up a business with signing an agreement, and I don't do anything with consulting my lawyer. I try to protect myself fully. I also learned to spend more time with my family. I go there every Saturday now, to have dinner with them, even if it's just for a while. And, of course, I learned to respect myself. I've never again let anyone humiliate me or treat me badly – because I'm a person. I'm a human being. Once, a client insulted someone on my team, and I called her to tell her we wouldn't work with her any more.

CK: Were you scared to start another business?

JC: I had some confidence problems as I was pretty emotionally battered, but I had no choice, because I can't just sit for eight hours a day tapping at a keyboard and then go home and switch off from work. I was tempted at times to work for other people, but as soon as I felt a little better, I saw that my path was as an entrepreneur, and to do what I liked, my way. I had some partners in other businesses, but I ended up getting out of them. I don't want partners. I'm good on my own.

CK: I've never had partners. I've never seen a partnership go well. It always ends in tears… Have your priorities changed over time?

JC: Life has given me some gifts wrapped in shitty packaging. Things that were tough but that helped to remind me of my values. You can learn from even the very worst things. Now I have a partner I've built a fantastic relationship with, and I feel that he is my family. And I've been thinking about starting a family. In the business, I try to do things that motivate me, because I know that's the only way I can motivate and help other business owners. I like helping people so much that when I'm delivering a course, I forget to have lunch! I think life is for learning, and I'm learning and growing more and more all the time. Although results are still important to me, I enjoy the process more. As Eduard Punset, the Spanish politician, said: you find happiness in the waiting room for happiness. It's not about success, it's about the journey; the excitement you feel along the way.

CK: What would you say to business owners having a hard time right now and trying to get through it?

JC: I'd tell them what I've been telling them since the start of the pandemic: circumstances don't define us. Situations happen, they last however long, then they go. It's circumstantial, and you have to see it that way and have perspective. If you're an entrepreneur, you're still an entrepreneur even if you're having a rough time of it. What we have to do is find solutions, look to inspirational examples, and not listen to that little voice telling us we failed. Because if you stay inside the problem, you won't be able to find the solution. Mindset is so important. Circumstances right now are making things hard, it's true, and we could even say the government has handled it badly – but we're responsible for our own futures. If you want it, and you work for it, you'll get it – no matter the circumstances.

I leave things on this optimistic message from Judit. Having met her in person (well, via Zoom), I can see that she's speaking from experience; from the knowledge she's acquired by getting through some hard times. She's a fighter, and in these difficult times, we all need to fight and to be inspired by people like her.

"

Judit Catalá: Situations happen, they last however long, then they go. It's circumstantial, and you have to see it that way and have perspective. If you're an entrepreneur, you're still an entrepreneur even if you're having a rough time of it.

JAN-ERIK OLSSON (1951)

www.linkedin.com/in/jan-erik-olsson-54606b1

20th June 2020.

In mid-2018, a Czech friend of mine, Pavel, was looking for an investor for a project of his: he wanted to create a bitcoin-euro bureau de change. He didn't need money to create the platform, but for running costs, since a business of that kind needs liquidity – it needs to have a certain amount of money in each currency. In his quest, he contacted Jan-Erik, a Swiss veteran businessman living in Spain (in the Arturo Soria area of Madrid).

They both supported the Czech government initiative of creating the Free Republic of Liberland, a micronation on the Balkan peninsula, between Croatia and Serbia. Pavel had chosen me as an external mentor or advisor for his project, and he asked me to go to his meeting with Jan-Erik. Though he ultimately decided not to invest in Pavel's business, we struck up a good relationship and have stayed in contact ever since.

Jan-Erik is a real veteran of the business world, and he's seen it all. I'm glad he's a part of the book, because he brings a touch of experience and serenity, unlike younger entrepreneurs like Jaime Chicheri and Judit Catalá, who are bubbling over with ideas and perpetually restless. Jan-Erik, although still very active at sixty-nine years old, exudes the kind of calm that comes with time and perspective.

He also has a highly international profile; he's started projects in the Baltic countries, Russia, Poland, Germany, particularly in the real estate sector but also in the trade of industrial and precious metals such as palladium, and financial instruments. He's an ardent liberal, like me. I guess that's why we get on so well.

We connect through Zoom, as usual. In the background of his webcam, I can see what I assume is his office: a wall lined with shelves stacked with perfectly ordered files, and another, lower shelf featuring family photos, a hardwood table and a leather armchair, which he is reclining on, looking relaxed. Despite his millionaire status, he's dressed very casually, not ostentatiously at all, in a simple navy blue T-shirt. This tells me that he doesn't like to spend his time on superfluous things, so I decide not to steal too much of it from him. Without further ado, I get straight to the point.

CK: What would you say has been your biggest failure as an entrepreneur?

JEO: I've actually had two. They happened almost at the same time, and they changed my life. I'll start with the more serious of the two, since it actually had some legal consequences. I remember that I was in Copenhagen and a man I knew contacted me, a Swedish businessman. In exchange for four million dollars, he offered to sell me the transport business of a Polish company that was part of a big Swedish brokers. They assured me it was all above board, but I said I wanted to visit the company in Sweden before accepting. They said, okay, but that I needed to sign a contract first so that they could take it to their bank the next day and get a loan for investing in the business. I agreed on the condition that they wouldn't use the contract until I had given the operation a once-over. I did it because I thought I knew them, and I trusted them. But two days later, when I traveled to Stockholm and met the company rep, he asked me for ten per cent of the four million in cash. According to the contract, I had to pay it within three days...and two days had already gone by. I called my lawyer and investigated a little, and we came to the conclusion that the supposed consignments from the Swedish company didn't exist. What that company actually did was pick up contaminated oil in Estonia and drop it in the Baltic Sea. It was a little more complicated than that, but I'll sum it up like that for clarity. I didn't want to be involved in illicit activity, so I refused to pay the agreed amount. The problem was that I had signed a contract, so the Swedish company took me to court for reneging. It seemed impossible that I would lose given all the documentation I had on them, but I did lose, and I was ordered to pay the four million dollars plus interest. So not only was the business a fraud, but I lost at the hearing, too.

CK: How long ago was that?

JEO: The first meetings were in 2008 and the hearing was in 2012.

CK: And nothing happened to them?

JEO: No, because by then the company didn't exist any more. The Swedish judge just saw that I had signed a contract promising to pay four million dollars, and that I hadn't done it. I'm sure he was in bed with them too, though: a corrupt judge. I felt totally defenseless and powerless. A lot of people seem to have this idea that Sweden is impeccable, including in a business sense, but it's not. There's corruption there, too, and fraud, and crime...

CK: What did you learn from that event?

JEO: Never to sign a document with carefully studying it and your future partners. Even if they seem like trustworthy people, even if you know them, you have to do your research or you could end up as the victim of fraud, like what happened to me. And it's not a matter of being naïve. I'd been doing business for many years when that happened.

CK: How long?

JEO: I started my first business in 1975, so when the Sweden thing happened, I'd been doing it for nearly thirty-five years. But you're never immune to fraud. There are unscrupulous criminals out there and you could come across one any time. Some of those criminals could be dangerous.

CK: Did you change anything about the way you are as a business owner after you had that experience?

JEO: I don't think so. What had happened was that I thought I knew some people, when I didn't really know them. I was too trusting. It's psychology, applied to business

CK: Were you angry, scared...?

"

Jan-Erik Olsson: Never to sign a document with carefully studying it and your future partners. Even if they seem like trustworthy people, even if you know them

"

JEO: Angry, yes – scared, no. I found out the Swedish guy had it all planned out, and that really made me mad.

CK: Did it affect your personal life at all?

JEO: No. The truth is that after so many years setting up companies, I already knew how to separate my private life from my businesses.

CK: That's something I find hard. I'm not good at drawing a line between my personal life and my business.

JEO: When you work for yourself, it's hard to distinguish between the professional and the personal, but you can stop business problems from affecting your private life. At least, I've managed it. In the business world, there are good and bad moments. In my case, over the course of forty-five years, you can imagine there's been all kinds. Show me a businessman who says everything goes perfectly and I'll show you a liar... or, at least, not a true businessman.

CK: A lot of people are having a bad time because of the Covid-19 crisis right now. Yesterday, I read that of all the street-level businesses that had to close because of the Spanish lockdown, thirty per cent won't reopen. And those that do will probably take some time to recover – if they ever do. What advice would you give to a business owner having a rough time of it now?

JEO: I'd tell them to try to lean on people around them who can help. In my case, I am enormously lucky enough to share it all with my wife, who is my better half. We can't carry the weight of everything on our own shoulders and think we can go it alone. Another tip would be to turn the page as soon as possible. What's done is done. You can learn from what you've been through, but if you dwell on it, you won't move forward. I've told you about my failures and hard times because you asked me, but normally, I don't even think about what happened. I stopped hurting from it a long time ago. I sleep easy at night now.

CK: You mentioned you had two particularly difficult moments. What was the other?

JEO: It happened at around about the same time. I hadn't done any business in Sweden for many years. A person I knew, the owner of a small real estate agency, called me and said: "Jan, could you do me a favor? I've been diagnosed with cancer and I have a year to live. And I want to get my life in order before I die. Can you buy my company out?" I did, and he died a year later. As part of the agreement we had come to, I had to maintain the person responsible for managing the property rentals. Through him, I got the chance to take on three hundred apartments in a Swedish town of around twenty-five thousand residents, near to where the company was based. Back then, in Sweden, the local government could deny a developer the rights to build or invest. In that specific council, the mayor was a communist, and didn't want me to take ownership of the apartments. Despite that, I decided to go ahead and we took it to court. It was stupid, because the apartments needed water, electricity, waste removal, and so on, and all of that depended on the council. So they made things as difficult for me as they could. It took us much longer than usual to restore the apartments, and we had a bunch of problems. And, of course, that meant I had to invest a lot more than originally foreseen. Then, I had big problems renting out the apartments, especially the renters' unions, which are very powerful in Sweden. I didn't know what was going on. I couldn't understand all the animosity toward me. First, the mayor refused to let me buy the apartments, and then the renters' union blocked my way. So, one day, I talked to someone from the union and I asked him outright what he thought of me. And his response chilled me: he considered me a good guy, but I lived in Spain. And that doesn't go down well in Sweden. Swedes love to help people from wherever, but not people who leave the country and live somewhere where everyone wants to live. So, I was a good guy, but I was still a Swede who had left the country to live in Spain.

CK: Whoa!

JEO: When I found that out, I did my numbers and realized I was losing a ton of money. I mean, we're talking about three hundred apartments here. Plus, I had debts to pay, because the property administrator wasn't paying, and the electricity company threatened to shut us off. The tenants took me to court because they considered that I'd lost ownership of the apartments. They colluded to get me out. And I had no choice but to declare the company bankrupt. This was in 2012, so it coincided with the hearing of the other problem I told you about.

CK: God, how did you manage to deal with all of that at once? How did you manage to keep it together?

JEO: Well, it was hard, of course. Those were difficult years, from 2006 to 2012, give or take. Everyone was against me purely because I was a Swedish person who had left for Spain. I was being punished for that. The mayor was smart and he knew what to do. Plus, there was a local reporter – probably associated with the mayor and the communist party – who was constantly trying to dig up dirt on me. And when he didn't find any, he invented it. That defamation hurt, because my family lives in Sweden. Without saying anything further, my daughter is a judge there.

CK: And did you talk about it with her?

JEO: No, I never talked about business with her or told her about that. I didn't want to put her in a difficult position. Fortunately, she has her mother's surname, so nobody made the link between her and me. That reporter used to write about me as if I were a criminal. He did me untold damage, because although I never did anything illegal, people just think there's no smoke without fire.

CK: How did you feel?

JEO: It ended up affecting my self-esteem and self-image, because it's tough to feel that kind of rejection. But I stopped dwelling on it a long time ago. Sometimes it darkens my mind, but it quickly passes. My conscience is clear, because I know I did things right.

CK: I guess that after those two experiences, you stopped doing business in Sweden, right?

JEO: Of course. There are people there who still won't talk to me, but my life is in Spain.

CK: From what I can see, you're still very active. Don't you want to retire?

JEO: The thing is: I like what I do. My wife – who, as you know, is a singer – sometimes gets asked the same question. And she replies: "I'll retire when I stop getting calls."

CK: Have your values changed over time?

JEO: In some respects. For example, when I was younger, I admired intelligent people; now, I admire kind people.

CK: One last question: how would you define success?

JEO: For most people, success is related to money. To me, money is important, I won't tell you it's not. I'd rather cry in a Rolls-Royce than a Volkswagen. But was success really means is achieving happiness, and happiness means being content with what I have.

CK: The simple answers are the best ones. Thank you for your time, Jan. I'm really happy to have you in the book. Love to your wife.

"

Jan-Erik Olsson:
Turn the page as soon
as possible. What's done
is done. You can learn
from what you've been
through, but if you dwell
on it, you won't move
forward.

"

DR. JULIAN HOSP (1986)

www.julianhosp.com
www.linkedin.com/in/julianhosp

16ᵗʰ July 2020.

It's been almost a month since I left Madrid. Now, I'm on my own with my other dog, Laia, living in a caravan camped next to the Picos de Europa mountain range. There are quite a lot of people here, since it's summer, and people have finally decided to leave the city or go on vacation. These past few weeks haven't been easy. From the pretty traumatic experience of being shut away in an apartment for over two months was compounded by the loss of my darling dog Kasia and the discovery that I've had ADHD my whole life and didn't know about it. All of this has caused me a kind of grief that it's taken me a few weeks to deal with.

During this time, I haven't really felt like carrying on with the book. It didn't seem important. I guess I've been depressed. But a few days ago, I realized it still makes a lot of sense to do it – the situation for business in Spain, especially small ones, is even more critical than at the start of the pandemic. So I've picked my pen back up.

Actually, I don't have much longer to go before I've fulfilled my plan: just a couple more interviews. Today's is with Julian Hosp. Julian was, in fact, the first person I asked to collaborate with me on the book. He didn't think twice. "Count me in," he replied. Then things got delayed – first on his end, because he was busy with the launch of a new product at one of his companies in Singapore, and then on my end, for the reasons I just explained. But today is finally the day.

I carry out the interview from inside the caravan; through videocall, as always. When my camera comes in, I see that I'm in silhouette, so I have no choice but to draw the curtain behind me and deprive Julian of the majestic panorama of the Picos de Europa.

It's been a while since he and I have talked. The last time we saw each other was in December 2019 in Frankfurt, where we held a meeting for his mastermind, ILG (meaning: Lions Group). Although he lives in Singapore, he's constantly traveling all over the world, just like me. In addition to his companies, he's a well-known speaker, especially relating to bitcoin and blockchain, which he's an expert in. His company, I-Unlimited (www.i-unlimited.de) manages his courses, talks, personal or professional development events, books, and generally everything relating to his personal brand.

He comes online and, as always, he looks slick, young, and dynamic. He looks ready to jump on his kitesurf board – he's been a pro at the sport for ten years. Looking at him, anyone would think he was Australian rather than Austrian. He's dressed casually, in a simple white T-shirt with a couple of bold accessories, like his neon blue watchstrap.

We speak in German, as we tend to do among ourselves. The first thing I ask him to do, as with the others, is tell us a brief history of himself:

JH: I'm from a little town near Innsbruck, in the Austrian Alps. I come from a very normal family. We weren't rich, but we didn't want for anything at home. My parents are still married. My mother was a teacher and my dad an architect. I have a sister two years younger than me, but we're not at all alike. I've always been a good student and find it easy to learn, while she shines more in social situations. Leave her with a group of strangers and pretty soon she'll be chatting to all of them. My intelligence is more analytical. I've always been good at math, and numbers in general. Why am I telling you this? Well, because when we were little, our mom wanted us to get the same results as each other, so she was much more attentive to my sister since she didn't get the grades I did. I was jealous of that, and I think that that gave rise to a somewhat competitive streak in me. I was eager to show my mother that I was better than my sister, and I wanted her approval in everything – right down to board games. So I forged this fighting spirit, which I still have. I couldn't stand to lose, and I still can't. If I'm playing a game against someone and I know I'm going to lose, I get upset and sometimes I even yell. My childhood could be summed up as: me against the rest of my family.

CK: So, you're a born competitor.

JH: I don't know if I was born that way or if it was nurture, but I definitely was and still am very competitive. Even now, if someone disagrees with me or expresses a different opinion from mine, I can't help arguing. But it's not a bad thing; it's just a reflection of my fighting spirit. Then, when I was a teenager, things changed a little, because at fifteen I went to the US to study for my high school diploma. My parents didn't want me to go that far away, but in the end, they accepted it – which I'm very grateful to them for. When I got there, I realized school was a lot different from in Austria. The level of math was really high, and I had to buck my ideas up, because there were other kids – even younger than me – who were better than I was. I studied hard and discovered that I could do more than I had thought I could. I realized that my limits were wherever I wanted them to be.

CK: A great realization to have.

JH: Yeah; it was key in my life. In fact, looking back, going to the States at fifteen was one of the most important decisions of my life. I had a good foundation, thanks to my parents, but it was on that trip that I discovered that I was the only thing that could hold me back. The sky is the limit. I'm not sure I would have ever achieved that mindset had I stayed in Austria.

CK: If I remember correctly, the reason you went to study in the US was to play basketball. How did that go?

JH: My plan was basically to play basketball with the best, and go pro. I had had an early growth spurt, and when I got there, I was one of the tallest kids. The problem was that I plateaued and didn't get beyond my current height, which is five feet eight. And it's hard to stand out in basketball at that height. I went from being one of the tallest to one of the shortest.

CK: So what did you do?

JH: I had to study something, and I decided on Medicine. Sometimes, looking back, I think we can be surprised at the decisions we made. That was one of the strangest decisions of my life. I was heavily influenced by the father of the family I was staying with in the States. To him, there were only two "real" kinds of career: Law and Medicine. He spent an evening explaining his theory to me, and in the end, I opted for Medicine. It wasn't a well-thought-out decision; I made it in one evening. Before I started the course, I went back to Austria to spend the summer with my parents, and I discovered a sport that wasn't very well-known back then: kitesurfing. This was in 2004. And I found that I was really good at it. I had good coordination, I was physically strong, and my height was an advantage there, so I got good fast. For a few years, I juggled my studies in Medicine with kitesurfing competitions, but there came a point where I had to choose: either stay in the States, or go back to Austria and become a professional kitesurfer. And I went for the latter. That was the second big decision of my life. It was risky, because although it's an Olympic sport now, it was little-known back then.

CK: Did you ever practice Medicine?

JH: Yeah, I practiced for a while, but I missed the travel and the freedom of kitesurfing. And the creativity. Also, I was annoyed by the bureaucracy and procedures involved in Medicine. With so much paperwork, I was spending very little time with patients. So, after a while trying in vain to adapt to it, I left the hospital I was working in. And that's a shame, because my grandmother would have liked to have a doctor in the family.

We laugh, thinking about Julian's grandmother.

JH: I had been mulling over the idea of quitting Medicine, when one day, a boy came in who had lost both arms in an accident. That's when I realized that life can change radically from one moment to the next, and that I should do what I really liked doing if I wanted to be happy. I remember that shortly after that I got on a plane to Lima, where a friend was waiting for me to do some kitesurfing there. It was during that flight that I decided to leave Medicine. When I landed, I told my friend, and he told me to quit over the phone – but I needed to do it in person. So I never even left the airport; I bought a ticket to Austria right then, went to the hospital, and canceled my contract. On the flight back, I felt freer and lighter than ever before. I wasn't afraid. I had endless ideas in my head about what I would do next. The only problem was outside pressure. So many people were telling me that I had done something insane. Luckily, I didn't listen to them.

Things went well for Julian after that, but not all the time. He tells me he had his problems, so I ask him to tell us about them.

JH: I had a lot of success with the kitesurfing. I didn't get to be number one in the world, but I was making good money. At twenty, I had around seventy thousand euros saved up. One day, I think it was in 2006, I met someone in Brazil who seemed well-connected, and we made friends. I had the ambition to make a lot of money, so I accepted his offer to buy a house by the sea, which he told me would appreciate in value quickly. I was happy because I thought I had found a great opportunity, so I transferred him the agreed amount…and I never heard from him again. He scammed me. And to this day, thirteen years later, the case is still open in Brazil.

CK: You had mentioned that to me before, but I didn't know the details.

JH: That was significant for me, not just because it upset me so much, but because it changed my relationship with money. I realized that my problem wasn't making it, it was keeping it. I wasn't making smart investments. With time, I've learned that it's important to diversify. Now I make fewer mistakes when investing, and when I do they're less serious. I still make the wrong decision sometimes – like everyone does – but they don't affect me so much.

CK: How did you learn?

JH: First I realized that instead of looking for someone to blame, I had to accept responsibility. I'm the one who made the decision, so I'm responsible for it. It's no one's fault and you can't go pointing fingers. That's the main thing: because some people go through life blaming everyone else, and that never turns out well. It was a process that lasted months, but in the end I realized I had to make my own decisions and be accountable for the results, whether good or bad. After that I started reading books on finance, like *Rich Dad, Poor Dad* and *The Richest Man in Babylon*. I've read a lot since them, because I'm convinced that knowledge is fundamental. The people around you are, too. Your surroundings are super-important, especially not having negative people around you who suck the energy out of you all the time. At the time that I got scammed, I was surrounded by people who partied all the time, even people into drugs. It was a short period, but I made some stupid decisions, partly due to the environment I was in. So I learned it's important to surround yourself with good people. And what's more, you have to cut off relationships with people who aren't good for you, people who hold you back. Now, I wouldn't hesitate to cut ties with someone who wasn't good for me or my goals.

CK: I always say we are the five people we spend the most time with…

JH: I don't know if it's five, but I agree with that. The important thing is that you have the courage to distance yourself from people if you detect any sign that they're not good for you – that they're toxic. There are always signs. I know it's not easy, but the best thing to do when you see those signs is to make fast and drastic decisions. In my case, when I need to get away, I go live in another country and change my environment completely. After I left Medicine, I left Austria too, and went to live in Hong Kong. Later, in 2014, I realized I needed another new chapter, so I went to live in Singapore. Most people are afraid of making radical life changes, even when they're deeply unhappy. Not me. I like quick solutions: ripping the Band-Aid off.

CK: There's nothing wrong with leaving things behind and dropping heavy baggage.

JH: Right. Some people criticize me because I'm very radical in that sense. I say: "If your family holds you back, leave your family." And they say, "How can

"

Dr. Julian Hosp: With time, I've learned that it's important to diversify. Now I make fewer mistakes when investing, and when I do they're less serious.
I still make the wrong decision sometimes – like everyone does – but they don't affect me so much.

"

I leave my family? That's inhuman." But I've done it, and it was good. At some point you need to cut the cord so you can grow. That doesn't mean they stop being your family, or your friends stop being your friends, but you distance yourself from them so you can do what you need to do to keep growing. You need to be honest with yourself and ask yourself: "Do I really want this life or should I let go and start walking on?". It's easier today than it was a few years ago. We have a lot of ways to stay in touch long-distance. If we want to, that is.

CK: Have you had a lot of failures as a businessman, apart from what happened to you in Brazil?

JH: I had a lot of problems in Hong Kong. I was there for two and a half years. I started a multilevel marketing business that got a lot of visibility and I was heavily criticized for that. It was hard to learn to deal with rejection from clients; not just "no", but aggressive behavior and insults. No one wants to work in sales, because you get a lot of no's, a lot of rejection. Learning to deal with that is one of the most important lessons to learn if you want to be successful in business. I usually describe that period in Hong Kong as "throwing spaghetti at the wall" – you try a bunch of stuff and not much sticks. That goddamn spaghetti gave us a lot of trouble. But that was the process we had to go through to become successful. It was a real lesson. I also learned you can't be as trusting as I was when it came to doing business in partnership with other people. A handshake won't do it. You need to know a person well, and above all, see how they treat others. Then, you need to sign a detailed contract that's been checked over by a lawyer. Whenever I haven't done things that way, I've run into problems.

CK: And what was it like after that, in Singapore?

JH: Great at first. I got really into blockchain, and, with a partner, I set up a project related to cryptocurrency: TenX. We raised one hundred million dollars in a single round of funding! But the relationship turned sour. Although I was the face of the project, my partner became greedy, and since he had made me sign a contract that was highly favorable to him, he ended up kicking me out of the business acrimoniously in early 2019. I took it hard. I spent a few days feeling really depressed. I wish I had handled it better, but…anyway, you live and learn.

CK: When you start up new projects, what's more important to you: the goal, or the process?

JH: I always set myself goals, but I enjoy the process, too. In fact, I think there are two main types of people: those who set goals and aren't happy until they reach them, and those who set goals and enjoy the journey, and love it, so that by the time they finally reach their goal, it doesn't really make them that much happier. I'm in the latter group. For me, my aim isn't the most important thing. What matters most is what I gain along the way: experiences, knowledge, new relationships, contacts to incorporate into my circle, and so on. Over time I've learned the importance of having a good network, of being well-connected. Learning and widening my circle is what's most important to me.

CK: Since you mention your network – I've seen

people criticizing you on social media. How do you feel about that?

JH: I try to deal with it, but I think I could probably do it better. It has three levels for me. The first is where you feel bad and you dwell on it. The second is where you ignore it. And the third, which I haven't got to yet, is when you manage to flip it around so that those negative opinions work in your favor. That's what people like Elon Musk do; he uses his haters to get more publicity. He goes on social media smoking a joint to provoke people into reacting. If you're smart, negative opinions can help get people talking about you and increase your renown; you reach a bigger audience. For example, when something negative gets published about my company, the next day, we have more clients. It's surprising, but that's how it is; it's a fact. And that happens because people read things, inform themselves, and come to their own conclusions, which are often positive ones.

CK: In Spanish, we use a phrase from Don Quixote: "*Ladran, luego cabalgamos*". It basically means that if people are criticizing you, you must be doing something right.

JH: Yes, I agree. Whatever people say to you, you have to keep moving forward. Because in reality, the only person who can beat you down is you. What other people say is only as important as you make it. I know that's hard sometimes, because we all want to be liked. When you see a negative comment about yourself, you wonder: why doesn't that person like me? But ultimately, you have to be practical and focus on results. If the results are where you want them to be, who cares what people say? There will always be someone who doesn't like you, or someone you don't get along with. That's just life. We're not tubs of Nutella.

We laugh about the analogy. It's true that Nutella is one of the few things that near enough everyone likes.

CK: You've had several books published, and some would say you're a business icon, especially when it comes to bitcoin and blockchain. Do you see yourself that way?

JH: I'm no guru; I just talk about my own experiences, about my thirty-four years of life. I can't advise anybody about things I haven't experienced myself. What is true, though, is that I like to share my experiences – for the exact reason I was saying before, which is that I truly believe in the importance of having a network and nurturing it. And to get, first you have to give. I offer ninety-nine per cent of my knowledge totally free. But like I said, I don't consider myself to be a guru or anything like that. I just talk about things I've done, my decisions, and my results – and always in the most objective and transparent way possible, so that each person can draw their own conclusions and see if they can apply it to their lives. If someone asks me about something I haven't experienced, I politely tell them I'm not the right person to ask.

CK: Are you satisfied with what you've achieved?

JH: Yes, very. I could have double the amount of money I've got by now if things had gone differently – if I hadn't been scammed or made certain mistakes – but I don't think that would have made me happier. There's not much difference between a million more or a million less. I live well, and, above all, I have projects and challenges I'm really excited about.

He smiles when he says this, and seeing him, I'm certain that he'll do big things (even bigger things, I should say), especially in relation to cryptocurrencies. And it's not just because he's still young; it's because I see in his eyes that he's still as competitive now as he was as a child. Now, of course, he's that much wiser.

"

Dr. Julian Hosp:
For me, my aim isn't the most important thing. What matters most is what I gain along the way: experiences, knowledge, new relationships, contacts to incorporate into my circle, and so on.

"

ALEXANDRE SAIZ (1975)

www.alexsaiz.com
www.linkedin.com/in/alexandresaiz

28ᵗʰ July 2020.

I'm still carrying out interviews from inside the caravan. I have two left: one today, and one tomorrow. That will complete the dozen that I set myself when I began this project.

I'm in the process of deciding whether to go on to France or stay a little longer in Spain, so I've decided to stay in Zarautz in the meantime, near to the border between the two countries. It's best to be prepared; I don't want to get locked down again. More and more outbreaks are happening and I really don't trust the various Spanish governments' management of this pandemic, from state level down to individual districts.

In a few moments, I'm going to be talking with Alexandre Saiz, a Catalonian entrepreneur based in Malaga, where he has a company: microapps. I haven't met Alex, as he likes to be called, in person, but I thought it would be interesting to ask him for his story, because his journey as an entrepreneur has been so interesting. He has gone from the construction business, where like so many others he was hit by the crisis of 2008, to the world of the internet and software. From brick to bit, as he explains in great detail in his latest book, *E-Business: How to Make Money on the Internet*, which talks about how to start up in the online world. The book, by the way, is available in Spanish, English, French, German, Italian, and even Catalan, Alex's mother tongue.

His previous book, *Multiply Your Sales With Amazon* (not yet available in English), touched on another very interesting topic for any business owner or self-employed worker: how to use the distribution giant to sell your own products. In it, he describes his experience of selling pet food over several years, first via www.telepienso.com, an online pet supply store, and then through Amazon, and he tells us the tricks he has learned along the way.

Alex is in Menorca at the moment, where he's trying to make something of the summer and make up for the months he spent shut away in his apartment in Malaga. When we connect, I tell him that my daughter Jacqui is now living in Malaga, too, with my ex-partner who is training to be a pilot. He tells me he has a daughter call Julieta, who's a little younger. It's strange: at this very moment, his daughter and mine could be walking past each other on a street in Malaga, not knowing each other, while he and I are talking via Zoom from Zarautz and Menorca respectively. It never fails to amaze me how big and small the world can be at the same time.

I thank him in advance for contributing to the book, and I ask him to tell us a little about his adventure as an entrepreneur – a term we both agree has been thrown around so much that its lost some of its original meaning (I personally prefer "business starter"):

AS: My family is from Vic, a city in central Cataluña. In fact, my parents and sister still live there. As in all of Cataluña, it's an area with a lot of entrepreneurial people, which I guess influenced me. In generally, Spain has quite a bureaucratic mindset, and it's often looked down upon to want to start up by yourself, but in Cataluña there's a long tradition of entrepreneurs, *botiguers*, etcetera. I'm talking about people who make a living without depending on the State. My parents weren't an example to me in that sense, as my mother is a retired teacher and my father worked in a toy factory. My mother is of Jewish descent, but I tend to think my entrepreneurial vocation was more a matter of personal ambition; of wanting to do better economically.

CK: When did you realize you had that calling?

AS: When I was small. By nine or ten years old I was going from door to door collecting empty cava bottles and selling them for scrap. I imagine they were later resold to bottling plants; there are a lot of them in Cataluña. That seems like just a little anecdote, but it was very significant. Looking back, I realize that with that simple activity, I was reaching the milestone every business owner faces: the first sale. When you achieve that, you realize you're capable of selling something. And that gives you a sense of power and confidence.

CK: That's true. Some people focus too much on developing their product because they're afraid of actually trying to sell it.

AS: Yeah, that's it. That's why I'm a great advocate for the "minimum viable product". I'll tell you more about it, but it's a philosophy I apply to all my software products: taking something that meets a need minimally and trying to find the first buyers for it. Because until you have buyers, you don't have a product. It's like a book: until it has readers, it's not fulfilling its purpose as a book Can you call an object nobody reads a book? Can you call an object nobody buys, or a services nobody uses, a product? I don't believe so.

CK: It's an interesting thought.

AS: After that early experience, I continued to develop a clear entrepreneurial spirit. When I was just thirteen or fourteen, I started getting interested in stocks. There were a lot of IPOs (Initial Public Offerings) in Spain at that time – I think it was under Aznar's government. Lots of big companies got floated, like Repsol and Telefónica. I wanted to buy shares, but I wasn't legally old enough, so I persuaded my parents' friends to give me their national ID numbers and I opened accounts in their name with Caixabank, which was called La Caixa back then. A friend of my dad's who worked there helped me manage it all. I would go see him in my lunch hour, because I was till at school. It went pretty well, I made a good amount of money out of it.

CK: I think it's amazing that at that young age you were interested in buying shares in big companies.

AS: I don't really remember where I got the information from: watching TV, I guess. I paid attention because I was interested in making money. As well as that, I did other things, like working on the weekends. My parents always encouraged my sister and me to earn our own money. For example, when we celebrated the festival of childhood and youth at Christmas, I would go to the council and offer to work as a supervisor. And on Saturdays I helped a local honey producer sell honey at the market in Vic. I don't even remember how I got talking to him. And I would go with some family friends to sell saucepans and frying pans at the weekly market in Granollers, a city near to Vic.

CK: Didn't it scare you to stand in front of customers and sell to them?

AS: I guess I got better at it as time went on. I've never stopped to analyze it in depth, but it's true that all those experiences helped to shape me. In a way, I think I was subconsciously absorbing everything that having a small business involves: pitching the products, speaking to potential buyers, invoicing, and so on. In reality, though, I didn't want to be a sales clerk. At that age, my dream was to get famous in a band I started with my friends. We even got hired to play some gigs, but that's as far as it went.

CK: This book talks about success, but it's mostly about failure, and how to overcome it. What would you say was your first failure?

AS: I remember one in particular from that period. I was at college, studying Translation and Interpreting, so I must have been nineteen or twenty. Me and a friend would hold college parties, and we made quite a lot of money. At one of those parties, just to give you an idea, we had over five thousand people at a sports pavilion and we took in twenty million *pesetas*, which was serious money. But anyway – around then, Terra came onto the stock market. It was an internet provider that looked as if it was going to be huge, and I invested almost everything I had made from the parties in shares in it. I think this was in 1999 or 2000. As soon as it was launched it went up drastically, over two hundred per cent, so it ended up on the IBEX 35 and barely three months later it became one of the top ten Spanish companies on the stock market. But then the dot-com bubble burst. The share price went from one hundred and fifty-seven to under three euros in 2005. Looking back, it seems obvious, but back then in the early noughties, Terra bought Lycos for twelve and a half million dollars. They looked like they were going to take over the world.

CK: Why did you study Translation and Interpreting?

AS: What I wanted to do was Journalism, but I didn't get the grades. And my mother suggested that I study Translation and Interpreting, because I was good at languages. In hindsight, it was a great idea, because now I operate in a world that's all in English: software development. Funnily enough, it was little like what happened to Steve Jobs when he studied typography at college: it was useful to him to give his Macintosh pretty, well-proportioned fonts, while English is useful to me now so that I can communicate with people from all over. My current company, microapps, has clients from dozens of countries and our workforce is like a microcosm of the UN. In fact, that's the whole philosophy of the start-up vibe nowadays: a mix of cultures and languages, but with one, universal one: English.

CK: What obstacles did you face when getting your first businesses off the ground?

AS: Not as many as now. In those early days, when

we did the parties and gigs, you just had to get a couple of permits and you were set. Now, you have endless regulations to comply with and paperwork to complete to do anything. Everything's become so bureaucratic. That's largely why I moved onto 'bits'; because things are easier online. You can create a product today and commercialize it all over the world in just a few days without having to jump through so many hoops. What I would tell entrepreneurs now is to get out there with the minimum resources they can and just get started. I don't mean break the law, of course, but if there's a piece of paper you need to submit in two months' time, just get started now and submit it when you can. You have to apply the whole *ask for forgiveness, not permission* thing.

CK: I completely agree with that philosophy. So what did you do after the college parties?

AS: A few parties didn't go that well and my investment in Terra failed, so I was heavily affected financially. My partner in the party business was okay, because he was a little more reserved, but I was really ambitious. Probably too much, looking back. I spent a summer learning German, and got hired by a company called Doctor Music, which organized some of the biggest music events of the time all over Spain, like concerts from Bruce Springsteen, Lou Reed, U2 and other big names. I was in charge of communication, particularly with the media. But I met a girl and my plan changed: we got married, and her dad, who worked in the financial sector, encouraged me to set up a real estate agency. It was still during the real estate boom; no one could have imagined that pretty soon, in 2008, everything would fall apart.

CK: I know exactly what you are talking about.

AS: We became partners and we started mediating in the buying and selling of apartments. That part of it went well. But not long later, driven by ambition and by the economic euphoria of the time, we decided to some real estate and run some promotions. My idea was to put more into the real estate services so we would get some regular income, which would have protected us when the crisis happened, but it wasn't just me. My partner was also my father-in-law, so I didn't have as much voice in decisions as I would have liked. Anyway, the crisis hit us hard.

CK: How did it affect you?

AS: Same way as most real estate companies. Suddenly, property you had bought for a hundred thousand euros wasn't worth more than ten thousand. It was insane. Most of our assets depreciated hugely. And not just that: I had no income of any kind, because the industry just dried up. So I had to reinvent myself.

CK: What did you learn from that time in the real estate sector?

AS: I did it for five years, and I learned a lot. One thing is that ambition can be a very poor advisor, and it can lead you to ruin. Another very important thing I learned is that you always need to bear in mind the worst case scenario and be prepared for it. You have to put situations on the table, even if they seem really unlikely. Sometimes you get so excited that your feet don't touch the ground, and you don't imagine any crisis could happen. But it's very useful to imagine and foresee them, because the most difficult part of being a business owner is getting through hard times. We're all prepared for the good times. I also learned it's very hard to get along with a partner, especially if they're family. You could be going at one pace and your partner at another; one of you has a wife saying to do certain things while the other one's wife says to do something else; one of you has one mindset and way of life and the other has another. And it's difficult to reconcile these differences and for them to drive the business forward. Usually, the opposite happens: they interfere in your day-to-day running.

CK: How did you go from 'bricks' to 'bits'?

AS: During the real estate boom, I had met several businessmen in the meat business, which is a big industry where I lived – the Osona region and its capital, Vic. A large part of the meat consumed in Spain is reared and slaughtered there. I was friends with some of them, and one suggested that I help him with a pet food line. I started up an online marketplace, www.telepienso.com, to sell this type of product. That's how I started selling dog and cat food all over Spain via the internet. At college, I was really attracted to the online world. In fact, as I was saying before, I had invested in Terra, which had a few internet portals. So when I saw that I had to reinvent myself professionally, I started exploring the internet more, and its endless possibilities.

CK: Was that when you created microapps?

AS: It happened very organically. Telepienso was built on an e-commerce platform called Shopify. It's a great platform, but I had to create a few specific developments, like a payment gateway in Spanish, which didn't exist. Then I saw that I could sell those developments to other e-commerce sites, and I started doing that through the Shopify appstore. I created a company for that business, and named it microapps. At first, it was a side gig, supporting telepienso.com, but over time it's become my main business. In recent years, we have created several tools that are sold worldwide; the internet has no borders. What's different about us is that the microapps developments are nearly always tools we need anyway, to improve our own services, and then we sell them to others who may need them too. Like MONEI: a payment gateway in Spanish, which now processes thirty million euros. Or Moonmail, which is an online marketing tool for sending out campaigns via SMS, e-mail, push, phone calls, and so on. We have around twenty thousand users now; some of which are surprising, like the Republican Party of the United States.

CK: You really make use of everything, then?

AS: Yeah; we Catalonians don't throw anything away, you know

CK: Hahaha.

AS: Jokes aside, that is precisely the philosophy: create something you yourself need, because that way you already have your first customer, and you know for sure your product meets a need or solves a problem. And if it works well for you, you can ask yourself if it could work for others, too. And always do it based on a Minimum Viable Product (MVP) which you modify based on user feedback as you go. I explain that in more detail in my latest book, E-Business. When that part of the software started to take off was when I really went from "bricks" – physical products – to "bits". Selling bits is a lot cheaper and less risky, as it requires less investment and you get fewer logistical problems. That said, you have to put in the hours to work out how the internet works and to be abreast of new developments, which isn't easy. I've had to learn programming concepts in order to explain to my developers what I want at each moment or to connect with really good people and get them working for me.

CK: You mentioned before that during your time in real estate, you learned you have to consider the worst case scenario and prepare for it. What else have you learned from your various experiences as an entrepreneur?

AS: A lot of things. One of them is that you have to get into as little debt as possible. The banks are great when everything's going well, but when it's not, they're ruthless. My biggest business failure, if you can call it that, was during the real estate crisis, and it largely happened because we had got into too much debt. Real estate is bad for that; you know that yourself. Since then, I've always been careful with my overheads and risks, and I've barely borrowed at all. If I can't afford something, I use my initiative to work it out, but I don't remortgage because you have to pay loans back, and with interest.

CK: Any other lesson you can pass on to other business owners?

AS: Yes. I've also learned that when it comes to reinventing yourself, don't discount anything, any possibility. When a door or a window opens, stick your head out and check out what's on the other side, even if it's not your area of specialism. You never know where life could take you, especially if you're open to surprises. Similarly, I've learned that in any activity, there's an element of chance. Sometimes luck may not be on your side – like when the real estate bubble burst – but sometimes it will, like when I started selling apps in the Shopify store and I was one of the first people in the world to do it. I got in with it when it wasn't very well-known yet, and then it became the second biggest e-commerce platform in the world, after Amazon but before giants like eBay. In business, as in life, there are things you can't control. We've seen that for ourselves with the pandemic. It was more or less impossible to foresee. But now that we know it's possible, we have to bear this kind of scenario in mind for the future. I've set my businesses up in such a way that, if circumstances were to change tomorrow, they could easily be repurposed or even dissolved with many problems. It's not what I want to happen, of course, but I'm ready just in case. I'm very aware that every business has a shelf life. And in the world of digital business, things change so quickly that what's great today could be worthless tomorrow. You have to be prepared to everything: including to disappear, when the time comes. At the end of the day, we're just bunches of cells floating round in the universe.

CK: You have to learn to let go and to keep perspective.

AS: In essence.

I find this last reflection of Alex's very interesting. In the same way that, in life, we try to avoid the topic of death, in the world of business many people also avoid the topic of failure or dissolution. As the Dalai

Lama said, "The western man lives as if he is never going to die, and then dies having never really lived."

CK: After everything you've experienced in your businesses, what is something you would never do again?

AS: Get into debt.

CK: Simple as that.

AS: Oh, and start a business with a partner.

CK: And what would you say to an entrepreneur going through a hard time right now?

AS: That I know exactly what they're going through, but that there are kids in Africa working at dumps ten hours a day, picking through trash to find something to sell so they can eat that day. I'd tell them to think about those kids and put their own misfortune into perspective. At the end of the day, we're animals, and we need just three or four basic things: to eat, drink, sleep, and not much more than that.

CK: One last question, Alex. What emotions did you experience when things went wrong for you?

AS: At times I was really scared I'd end up with nothing, but then I realized there's always a way out, especially if you're careful and you don't take more risks than you have to. Also, if you take care of your relationships with people, you'll always have a good friend or relative to lend you a hand if things get really ugly. I've also experienced how difficult it is to deal with uncertainty. For example, when you've been breaking your back over a project for months and it's not taking off, and you don't know whether to pack it in or keep going... That side of starting up businesses, especially if you're doing it alone, is hard – and no one talks about it. We only talk about the good bits, the successes, how cool it is to be an entrepreneur. I've also felt sadness at times, when I've lost friends over differences of professional opinion. But apart from that, I try to keep my emotions far away from my businesses. I guess it helps that I have quite a fun view of business. I see it kind of like a game that you should enjoy. Not to gamble like crazy, of course, but you have to accept that some you win and some you lose. I mean: some projects will work, and others won't. It even sometimes happens that what you thought would work doesn't, and what you weren't banking on ends up being your biggest triumph. Life is surprising like that. And business is a part of life.

Alex is meeting some friends for lunch, so we end it here. He says goodbye from the bathroom, where he's getting ready for his lunch date. He kindly offers to complete his answers or reply to any other questions, but I don't think it's necessary. Not only is he clear on what he means, but he expresses himself with total clarity. It's been a great chat.

"

Alexandre Saiz:
At times I was really
scared I'd end up with
nothing, but then I
realized there's always
a way out, especially if
you're careful and you
don't take more risks
than you have to.

"

DEBBIE-ANN GOHRT (1972) Y DANIEL PYKE (1975)

www.apkk.ca
www.supremaventures.com
www.linkedin.com/in/debbie-ann-gohrt
www.linkedin.com/in/danielpyke

29th July 2020.

As I explained in my introduction, the start of the pandemic caught me in Madrid and put the kibosh on my travel plans to Canada, where I was going to stay with some friends. Those friends are Debbie and Daniel: my interviewees for today. Instead of being with them in Montreal, we're meeting through a screen; they're in their home, and I'm in my new caravan.

I'm really excited to finish the book on them, as they're a great example of an entrepreneurial couple who support each other through hard times. As they've both lived through business disappointments first hand, they have the necessary empathy for understanding the difficulties involved in getting your own business off the ground.

They look great: happy, calm. They're dressed very casually: matching simple black T-shirt. I realize that something common to near every entrepreneur is the freedom to dress however they want at any time, without dress codes.

I begin by explaining the idea behind the book to them in a little more detail. I notice complicit smiles between them when I mention that they'll be able to check the interview over to make sure nothing too personal or intimate goes into the book. I see a great affinity between them.

I tell them I want to show the hidden face of that cool, mythical image of starting up a business that the media shows. The difficulties, the mistakes, the failures… And, of course, how people overcame them and what they learned. Because in reality, we should all be supporting each other, even if it's just by admitting our mistakes and sharing what we did when times were hard. That way we can find the silver lining to this pandemic that has knocked us all for six.

Daniel speaks first:

DP: Debbie and I are married, and our views on business are similar. We both knew from the start that we didn't want to work for other people. I tried a few jobs, but I couldn't stick it. I liked learning and I was motivated by new challenges, but as soon as the challenge was gone, I felt the urge to move on. I never lasted longer than eight months in a job…

DAG: I was even worse. I had to change jobs every week.

DP: I was very clear that I didn't want a boss; I wanted to decide for myself. I didn't know where to start, but that wasn't a problem. I don't think you have to limit yourself to just one thing. I see our kids getting asked at school what they want to do for the rest of their lives, and I think: "I'm forty-five, and I don't even know yet…". Since I started, I've founded fourteen businesses, which I've closed, sold, and so on. At first, they were small businesses based around simple services like dog-walking. You might not think that's a business, but where we live there are now dog-walkers who earn as much as lawyers do. The problem I had was that I could never take our businesses to the next level, and escalate them. There was always some obstacle: a new government regulation, needing specialist equipment, et cetera. So I would choose to close that business and start a new one. It was a pretty unstable situation. My first wife worked an office job, and she wasn't comfortable with the situation; she preferred the stability of a job with a monthly paycheck. And I couldn't do that; I needed to feel that I could grow. I wanted to grow!

CK: I understand.

DP: So I invested a lot of money in a marketing course: around seventy-five thousand dollars. That was the beginning of my divorce, because my wife didn't agree with that investment. But I insisted, and I did it. I thought that after that course, clients would consider me an expert, and pay me a lot of money to help them with their marketing…but it didn't work out that way. I had no experience, so I had nothing. Looking back, I can see that it was a good investment, but at the time I felt like a failure: my marriage was on the rocks, I had spent seventy-five thousand dollars on a marketing course, and I had no customers. After the divorce, I met Debbie, my lovely wife…

CK: Can you tell us your story, Debbie?

DAG: I was a good student my whole life: always focused at school, and later at college. But when I graduated and got my degree, all I found was office jobs where I had to do things I hated doing. One day, I saw an ad in the newspaper to get certified as an Early Years educator. I thought, "I don't really like being around kids – I'm not even sure I want to have any – but if I do this, I could get hired at a daycare." And I did: I started working in a daycare. I didn't really like it, but the money was good and I didn't have to work weekends. My working day finished at six on the dot. But over time, I got a hernia from working with little kids and lifting things. I had an operation on my back and I had to leave my job at the daycare. Then, my father started encouraging me to open a dry cleaners. What he actually did was buy a dry-cleaning machine and say, "You're going to have a dry cleaners." That's what happened. But during the first year of the business, I fell pregnant with my first son, Jonathan. My father was not happy about that at all. Two weeks after giving birth I was back at the dry cleaners. I took the baby with me to look after him there. And something strange happened: since I had my son in the back with me, a lot of customers started asking me if I had set up a daycare and if I was accepting kids. And that's how I started looking after some of the young children of customers at the dry cleaners.

CK: That's great! That's what I call listening to what customers want…

DAG: Yeah, it all started because I needed it myself, but then I saw that other families did, too. More people ended up coming for daycare than for dry cleaning. It worked really well until we got a letter from the Government telling us it was illegal. I couldn't have more than six kids...and I had forty! So we decided to change the whole thing, and fully replace the dry cleaning with daycare. We had to invest three hundred thousand dollars. Everything had to be checked over by an architect, and then the government came to measure up to make sure the space was suitable.

Daniel interrupts her, indignant about how much control the government had.

DP: They made a wall that went two inches into a room...two inches! The inspectors measured it and said, "You have to take two kids out of this room." Taking two kids out of the room meant losing twenty thousand dollars a year. And twenty years have passed since they did the work, so by now, that would be four hundred thousand dollars. For two inches!

CK: Yeah, that's crazy.

DAG: Anthony, our second child, grew up in the daycare. And then Thomys, too. I didn't take more than two weeks' maternity leave with any of them.

CK: In the movies, in the back of dry cleaners they usually have alcohol, or drugs, or...

DP: We had illegal kids.

We all laughed about this story.

DAG: To tell you the truth, I'm tired of the daycare now. The only good thing was being able to work and keep my kids with me. That was important to me. As I didn't have the luxury of being able to raise my kids at home, at least I could have them with me at work, and that made me happy. But it's been a very difficult business, because my mother was part of it too, and she had no business sense. My dad did, but he died in 2008. And since then, everything's been complicated.

CK: A lot of gurus will tell you: "Follow your passion". But sometimes your passion isn't profitable, and you have to put food on the table. We need money to live.

DP: Many people start businesses based around what they're passionate about, but a business is a complex thing. Debbie loves finger painting with the kids, but she also has to manage the maintenance of the premises, sixteen workers, a government that does constant inspections, and so on. And everyone goes to her with their problems. That's not easy, and it's not fun, either. That's why a lot of companies fail: because the person stopped doing what they love.

CK: I think there's something that goes beyond passion: purpose. Passion is great and all, but purpose is about what we should be doing with our lives, right?

They both agree.

CK: Debbie, how have you managed to do something for twenty years that you don't like? I don't think I could do it…

DAG: I do it because I know the business is our stability, our income. And it still works. I'm not yet at a point where I can take a break to think about what else I want to do. Plus, it's a way of supporting Daniel, who has a lot of great ideas and always tries to start up new and different things. Right now, we need the stability of the daycare.

DP: Normally, the guy is the stable one in the relationship. He goes out and earns the money that gives the family stability. That's not the case for us. Anyway, my hope is that one day I can give Debbie the chance to do what she wants to do.

CK: Debbie, you say you're not happy with the business. Does that mean you view it as a failure?

AG: No. As a business, it's successful. We turn over a million dollars a year, and now we're opening a second daycare next door, in the same building. So, despite the difficulties and the government obstacles, it's a success. We've had clients who stayed with us for five years despite competition. But we've had to get very involved – not just me, but Daniel and the kids, too. Being your own boss is fantastic, but what people don't see is that for the past twenty years, we've been working twelve hours a day, seven days a week.

CK: How do you handle your mother being a part of the business?

DAG: It's an ongoing discussion. We have very different criteria. She's afraid of any change, any investment that could make the business grow. She's holding us back. And it's very frustrating that she doesn't listen to us when we try to explain to her that to grow a business, you have to invest. Plus, every family dinner becomes a business meeting. It's hard when family is involved.

CK: I can imagine. But you two support each other?

DP: I try to. I have my own projects, but whenever she needs me to help out with the daycare, I do. It's a priority to me for Debbie to be able to delegate some responsibility; shift at least a little of that weight off her shoulders. And similarly, she supports me with all my crazy ideas, hoping that one day I'll hit the jackpot and earn ten, or twenty, or a hundred million dollars, and I can just take her right out of it. Because she works really long hours, and she's stressed. I'd like her to be able to wake up in the morning and say, "You know what? I'm not going to the daycare today, I'm going to chill out, or book our next trip."

CK: Has it all affected your relationship?

DP: Yeah. It's like there's no time for romance, because you're constantly building the business. There's no time for candlelit dinners, wine and cheese. What we do is work hard and pray to God that we earn enough to enjoy at least some years of our lives.

This sounds dramatic, but Daniel is laughing as he says it. I can tell that, despite the difficulties and the lack of time for romantic dinners, they share goals and understand each other.

CK: Daniel, you mentioned that once you set your ideas into motion, you get bored of them and want a change. Why do you think that happens to you?

DP: I think there are a lot of factors. For one: motivation. When I was dog-walking, I stopped one day and thought: "God, is this what I'm going to be doing for the rest of my life? No, I can't." and the lack of motivation drives me to change. Also, there's the income. At times I've found myself wondering: "Is this going to give me the million dollars I dream of retiring with? Will it get Debbie out of the daycare?" And if the answer is no, I change. I normally do a balance sheet on my birthday, not on January 1st, like a lot of people do. That day, I get up and reflect on how the past year has been: if I've moved forward or back. All the businesses I've started up have always reflected my will to be where I want to be.

CK: Have you ever wondered if you change businesses so much because you have ADHD? I found out recently that I've had the disorder for a long time, and that's shaped me in everything, including in how I do business.

DP: I don't know much about that disorder.

CK: I'll send you some information. I've found out a lot of things lately. It affects more people than you'd think. For me, it's been a positive discovery, because now I can understand why I sometimes need to switch off from other people or change places. Or change my life: start over. That's actually the title I'm thinking about giving the book. I need to have peace and silence. I'm a sociable guy, but sometimes I need to be alone.

DP: What you're saying does resonate with me. I'd like to take a look at the information.

I tell him I'll send it to him later on. I'll have to select just a few things, though, because I've compiled a huge amount of information on the topic recently.

CK: Going back to the interview, of the fourteen businesses you've set up, how many were successful and how many weren't?

DP: Financially speaking, they were all failures, because they didn't grow to where I wanted them to. But on the other hand, they were a success, because they made me who I am. I didn't go to college; I studied to high school, so I've had to learn from experience. All my businesses have been learning experiences.

CK: Are there any you've been particularly proud of?

DP: Yeah, my ice hockey school for goalkeepers. It was a success for several reasons: because I'd never played hockey, because our kids learned a lot there, because I ended up with six hundred customers, and so on. It also went well financially. And emotionally, because it was a way of connecting with our boys, who play really well, too. It was probably the best thing I've done. But my son Jonathan wanted to run the business his way, and he set up his own academy behind my back. He thought he could do a better job. He got ambitious, and within three days, he'd taken all my customers. It was a business with a lot of potential; it probably could have fulfilled my dream of letting Debbie retire and creating a family business involving his brothers, but my eldest son took it from us.

CK: Whoa. That's rough.

DP: Yeah, family...My mistake was never thinking that could happen. We didn't talk to Jonathan for a year, and neither did his brothers. And in the end, he quit the business, because he didn't know how to manage it.

CK: Maybe you could pick it back up...

DP: No, the whole experience left a bad taste in my mouth.

CK: What lessons have you learned from your experiences? Maybe that it's better not to mix business and family?

DP: Yeah, that's one. As parents, we want to make our kids' lives easier than ours were, but we forget that life is never easy. Business is never easy. I mean, every time you overcome a problem, you gain in confidence. It's true that we're tired because of the problems we were talking about, but we know that if we stick together and we're a team, then we can find a solution by putting our heads together. I've also learned you can't do everything alone; you need a team of people and to rely on others. It can be hard to build a team of trustworthy people, but you have to try.

CK: Now that you've had to close several businesses, are you afraid when it comes to starting up a new one?

DP: Afraid? No, because I have no choice. Looking for a job isn't an option. Although some businesses haven't gone well, it's all been a learning experience: that's the way I see it.

CK: What advice would you give to an entrepreneur starting out now?

DP: That when something doesn't work, think about what's stopping it from moving forward. Do some research and find a way to resolve it before carrying on. If I'd done that when I was twenty-two, things would be different for me today.

CK: And what would you both say to a business owner or self-employed person who's having a hard time right now because of the coronavirus?

DP: I would say that any problem you have in life, as long as it's not a terminal illness, you can overcome it. Just find the reason why you need to overcome it: your internal motivation, your greatest desire, your purpose.

DAG: I'd tell them to find that motivation and keep pushing, pushing, pushing. Try something different, something they haven't done yet. And don't waste time thinking about how bad things are: open their eyes and look around. There's only one thing to do: get up and keep going. In the end, there's always a way.

DP: Yes, and they should surround themselves with good people: friends, family, their partner. As long as their partner supports them, of course – because a lot of entrepreneurs don't have their partner's support, and they can feel really alone. But if you have positive people around you, you'll always find support: someone to help you see things from another point of view and to find your way.

CK: I think that's great advice.

I thank Debbie and Daniel for their time and their honesty. I'm sure their testimony will be really helpful – especially for any entrepreneurs feeling alone and misunderstood.

"

Debbie-Ann Gohrt:
Open your eyes and
look around. There's
only one thing to do:
get up and keep going.
In the end,
there's always a way.

"

"

Daniel Pyke:
I've also learned you
can't do everything
alone; you need a team
of people and to rely on
others. It can be hard to
build a team of trust-
worthy people, but you
have to try.

Epilogue

31st July 2020.

At the time of writing this short goodbye, out-breaks of the virus are on the rise all over Spain. More than four hundred of them. In some regions, such as Cataluña, they're already talking about the possibility of locking people down again. That would be terrible!

I think I'm going to cross the border today. If there's one thing that terrifies me, it's being confined again, and being told what to do. I value my freedom of movement where and how I want above all else – respectfully and responsibly, of course.

Writing this book has been a great experience. Not only have I learned from the experiences of other business owners, but I've discovered things about myself I didn't know, like the ADHD thing. I can finally put a name to something I've always had something of a complex about: my inability to concentrate on one ac-tivity for long, my perpetual restlessness, my lack of sleep, my need to start new projects all the time that I quickly get bored of and lose interest in; my need to move around every month or two, to see new landscapes and meet new people. Now, I'm learning to manage it so that it's not detrimental to me or to the people I love.

It's been an unexpected benefit of writing this book, which I began writing with the simple desire to help entrepreneurs having a bad time through this crisis. Once again, I'm seeing that when you give, you always end up receiving, one way of another. As Cipri said in his interview: "Some people might think giving has nothing to do with business, but for me, the best business is giving. To give is to add: it's to turn yourself into part of the solution, rather than being part of the problem. It's investing in people's hearts." And it's so true!

Despite the difficulties we're experiencing in these complicated times, I want to send out a positive message. As you've seen, all the business owners I've interviewed got through difficult, sometimes dramatic, times, and came out the other side. That's why I want to encourage you to keep fighting. Don't lose your entrepreneurial spirit. And preserve your freedom and autonomy; the State can help from time to time, but we business owners always end up paying for that help somewhere along the way (and with interest!).

Now is the time to look to the future. And, even more than that, to look closely at your reality, and use the circumstances in your favor. That's what a businessman I read about a few days ago did: he has a textile factory where clothes were manufactured, and now he's repurposed it to make face masks. A real example of adaptability.

I also recently read in *Cinco Días*, a business and finance newspaper, that big companies like McDonald's, Starbucks, Apple, Tesla, Uber and Airbnb were born during hard times for the economy. That's because in hard times, needs arise that provide opportunities for entrepreneurship. Airbus, Microsoft, Apple and Starbucks were founded in the seventies, against a backdrop of inflation, unemployment, and zero economic growth. And Airbnb was created right in the middle of the subprime mortgage crisis!

Times of change and uncertainty pave the way for new ideas and new proposals. There are a lot going on right now – in the health sector, for instance. The important thing, aside from staying calm, is to see a business opportunity where others see a problem. That's the right attitude. I know you might be afraid, but fear, like crises, can be overcome.

One journey ends here – but another begins. Today I'm going to hitch the caravan to my car and go on my way. I don't know exactly where I'll go, but I'm not worried about that. As Julian Hosp said in his interview, there are two types of people: those who set goals and aren't happy until they achieve them, and those who set goals and enjoy the journey. Like him, I belong to the latter group. For me, the destination isn't as important as the journey. And there's a journey for as long as there's a road.

 Christian Korwan

Remember you can find more exclusive content at::

www.christiankorwan.com

Acknowledgements

I want to thank all the friends who agreed to participate in this book and share their testimony with us. Thank you for being so open and describing your experiences to us, the good and the not-so-good, and for sharing what you've learned. It's been a pleasure to go on this little journey with you all.

Thank you to my parents, wherever they are, because they gave me a foundation that has allowed me to come out on top, despite my many obstacles, and to rise from the ashes of failure.

Thank you also to my daughter, Jacqui, whose very existence has pushed me to overcome the hardest of times.

Thank you to Eli and Lau, who have accompanied me through countless projects, for their patience, understanding, and loyalty. Thank you to everyone who has stayed by my side through difficult times.

And thank you, finally, to all the brave people who have dared to start up a business and who are battling to keep it afloat. This book pays homage to your determination, your hard work, your passion, and – above all – your dreams, without which humanity would still be living in caves.

From the bottom of my heart,

Christian.

Printed in Great Britain
by Amazon

77201414R10120